CALLED
BY
ANOTHER
NAME

A MEMOIR OF
THE GWANGJU UPRISING

DAVID LEE DOLINGER
WITH MATT VANVOLKENBURG

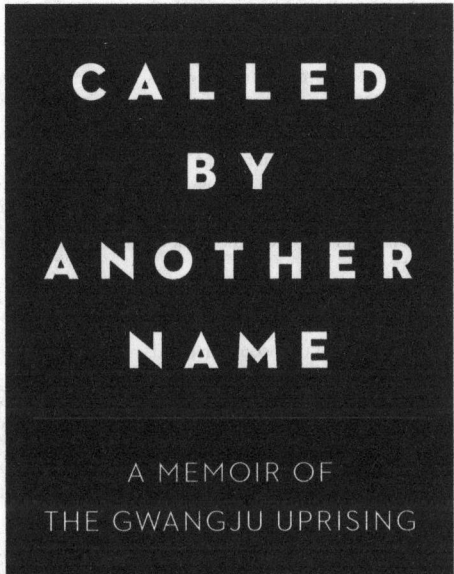

CALLED

BY

ANOTHER

NAME

A MEMOIR OF
THE GWANGJU UPRISING

Called by Another Name

Published by Goggas/Gaek
Anyang-si, Gyeonggi-do, Korea
phone +82 70 8019 0433
contact@goggasworld.com
www.goggasworld.com

Medway, MA, USA
phone 508 598 8366

ISBN: 979-8-9856069-9-7
Library of Congress Control Number: 2022904866

The Korean government changed its system for Romanizing Korean in 2000. Prior to this, Gwangju was written as Kwangju. To correspond with my memories of the events of 1980, I use its former spelling in the pages that follow.

As well, I have not capitalized "south" Korea and "north" Korea because these are not their official names and I believe that there is only one Korea, which I hope to see reunified in my lifetime.

Dedication

I dedicate this book to my wife and son, as they would have it no other way. But more importantly, I dedicate it to those who have fallen before me, who I remember each day with tears in my eyes. To all of those who have helped me through this life. To my extended Korean family and friends who have provided me with great warmth and support. To Park So-young, for dealing with my quirks. To Sue and Randy Rice, who knowingly or unknowingly gave me focus and support. To all of those who supported me and put up with me as a Peace Corps Volunteer in Yeongam. But mainly to Tim Warnberg, who I wish was still here, with whom I wish life had allowed me to stay in closer touch. I have been lucky in my life to meet many wonderful mentors, interesting and dedicated people, and very good friends. Each one of you in one way or another has helped me to reach the goal of publishing this memoir. Please know that I am always here for you as you have been for me.

Contents

Authors' Notes

David Dolinger

This book has been a long time coming, and for that I am sorry. I cannot adequately explain why it has taken so long. Partly it is due to me not living in the past, because of the pain I find there, and not worrying about the future, as it is the moment that counts. I was never afraid to speak about the Kwangju Uprising, and gave talks, interviews, and testimony about it in the 1980s after my return to the United States. There I worked with various organizations focused on exposing the truth about 5.18 (as the Kwangju Uprising is also known) and on human rights in the Republic of Korea. This work continued until the 1990s, by which point south Korea had made major strides toward democracy. After that I turned my attention toward my wife and son, and on trying to make a difference in the field of healthcare.

I have long wanted to write this book, and have had drafts of it written since the mid-1990s, but, due to my hectic schedule as a graduate student, writing my thesis, pursuing post-doctoral studies, and then concentrating on my family and my career, I never found the time to concentrate on it or finish it. It was not until 2005, when I returned to south Korea and Kwangju for the first time since 1981, that I realized it was time to renew my efforts to share my story. As George Orwell put it, "Who controls the past, controls the future: who controls the present, controls the past." Only those of us who are willing or able to tell our stories can shape the present, and, with this realization, I started down the path to sharing the story of what happened during the Kwangju Uprising from my viewpoint.

Over the years I have stayed up to date on developments in south Korea and on the literature surrounding the Kwangju Uprising, which I have found interesting but also, at times, disturbing. In the case of the Kwangju Uprising, it appears that the survivors have been able to share the story of what happened based on their own experience, observations, and stories they have heard. On the other hand, we also have histories written by former U.S. government officials stating that they were helpless to stop what was happening in Kwangju or moderate the Korean authorities' behavior in its aftermath. What is most unfortunate is that the honored dead of the Kwangju Uprising cannot tell us their stories. They cannot share with us what they were thinking and feeling, or why they died or were willing to make the ultimate sacrifice.

During my time living in Yeongam, South Jeolla Province, and during the time I spent in Kwangju in May 1980, the people I met and the friends I made did not call me David, but Im Dae-oon, the Korean name I was given at the start of my Peace Corps Training. Ever since, I have had two names, and still use Im Dae-oon whenever I visit Korea. During the time I witnessed—and participated—in the Kwangju Uprising, an event which changed my life and guided me down my life's path, I was called by another name, a name as important to me as the one I was given at birth.

Matt VanVolkenburg

When I first came to Korea in 2001, I quickly grew interested in Korea's modern history, and one aspect of it that most caught my attention was the Kwangju Uprising. When I started my blog, *Gusts of Popular Feeling*, in 2005, several of my earliest posts were about the Kwangju Uprising (also known as 5.18).

It was around that time that I read the book *Contentious Kwangju: The May 18 Uprising in Korea's Past and Present*, which featured a chapter by Jean Underwood about the experiences of American missionaries living in Kwangju in May 1980. In an endnote, she briefly mentioned something I had not known about—the involvement of Peace Corps Volunteers—and mentioned the names Tim Warnberg, Judi Chamberlin, and David Dolinger.

In 2006, during a discussion about the Kwangju Uprising on another blog, a former Peace Corps Volunteer who was taking part announced that he was going to invite to the conversation a fellow PCV who had witnessed 5.18 named David Dolinger. I immediately recognized David's name from the previously mentioned book and asked him a number of questions. In the years that followed, David left numerous comments on my blog about his experiences in Kwangju in 1980.

In the spring of 2013, two friends mentioned to me that David was living in Seoul. At that year's Royal Asiatic Society garden party, held at the British ambassador's residence, I began talking with someone who introduced himself as a former Peace Corps Volunteer who had lived in South Jeolla Province in the late 1970s. I was about to ask him if he had known David when I suddenly realized who I was speaking to!

We met a few times after that and discussed his experiences in the Peace Corps and during 5.18. During one of our conversations, I asked David if he had thought of writing about his experiences. He told me that he had, but that he would need help, since he was not a writer. I thought it could be an interesting project, but David soon left Korea to move to Switzerland, so the idea was put on hold for several years. In 2019, with the 40th anniversary of 5.18 approaching, David asked me if I would be interested in working with him on his memoir, and I said yes. By the end of that year, he had sent me a first draft, and throughout 2020 and early 2021 we supplemented what he had written with material gathered from Skype interviews and a steady exchange of emails, which was also the medium through which we revised the text. We supplemented David's memories with archival research, one result of which was an article I wrote for Volume 94 of *Transactions of the Royal Asiatic Society*-Korea titled, "Tell the World what is Happening: The Americans who Witnessed the Kwangju Uprising."

Though I've read about 5.18 for two decades, I learned a great deal by helping David tell his story. Not only is David's experience of 5.18 unique, in part due to his interactions with the student leaders in the Provincial Capital, but he also described the process of Peace Corps training in Korea (something I don't think has appeared in any other book) and shared the inspiring story of his involvement with Korean dissidents and the foreign missionaries who were helping them.

I hope readers get as much out of reading about David's experiences as I did in helping him put them on the printed page.

MAP
SOUTH KOREA / JEOLLANAM-DO

Chuncheon

Gangwon-do

Gimpo
Airport

Seoul

Gyeonggi-do

Chungcheongbuk-do

Chungcheongnam-do

Cheongju

Gyeongsangbuk-do

Jeollabuk-do

Daegu

Gyeongsangnam-do

Kwangju

Jeollanam-do

Jeju-do

Kwangju

Naju

Mokpo

Yeongam ▲ Wolchulsan

MAP
KWANGJU

Kwangju Train Station

Tim's Place

Geumnam-ro

Bus Terminal

MBC

Sangmugwan

Provincial Capital Building

Fountain

YMCA

Chonnam University Hospital

Daedo Hotel (Journalists' Inn)

Preface: One Night in May 1980

I slowly started to force my eyes open. No, I thought, close your eyes and focus on overcoming the discomfort. Stiffness had crept through my body. It dawned on me that I had nodded off in the uncomfortable, poorly padded chair. After gradually untwisting myself, I felt like I had control over my limbs again.

My brief nap had done little to help me overcome my exhaustion. I had my glasses on, but they didn't help much as I tried to take in my surroundings. The only sources of light were a burning cigarette and a strange glow coming from something I couldn't quite make out. It took a moment for the fog to lift and remember where I was.

It was sometime after midnight on Sunday, May 25, 1980. I was in the library of the Provincial Capital building in Kwangju. The strange glow was coming from a military radio. Earlier I had witnessed one of the daily update meetings held elsewhere in the same building. I had been asked to help monitor the radio, as it was thought that the government troops might use English to issue orders when they attacked Kwangju. Over the past few days there had been daily—if not hourly—rumors that the military was attacking or was tightening its noose around the city.

Through the glow I could make out the two other people who were monitoring the radio with me. One was a college student, and the other with the cigarette was a middle-aged man, a retired Korean army master sergeant.

We had been at our post since darkness fell on Saturday night. There had not been much chatter, and there was nothing in English, but it gave me a chance to listen to my companions' stories. They had also witnessed what was happening in Kwangju and had seen what the paratroopers had done to people. One told me he had seen no alternative. He couldn't just sit and watch—he had to do something. That was a common thread in the conversations I had had with people in Kwangju over the past few days. No one could sit back and do nothing, including myself, even though I was just a naïve, young Peace Corps Volunteer.

Sitting in front of that radio, listening to their stories, I could only wonder: How did I get here?

I asked myself that question many times during the events of May 1980. I asked it on May 16 as I listened to plans for the student-led torchlight march later that night, I asked it on May 21 as I walked into the city, I asked it that early morning on May 25, and I will probably ask it until the end of my days. I never realized where it would all take me, or how it would all fit into a journey of a lifetime.

Part I

There is Always
a Beginning

1. The First Steps of the Journey
January to June 1978

When I landed at Gimpo Airport on the morning of April 21, 1978, with my fellow Peace Corps trainees, I thought I knew what was in store for us. We were to be bussed to Cheongju to undergo ten weeks of language and tuberculosis control training before being sent to our assigned postings at health centers throughout the country. Things started off as planned. After descending the stairs from the plane and walking across the tarmac into the airport building, the specially issued passports the Peace Corps had arranged for us allowed us to breeze through immigration control. We were greeted by Leo Pastore, country director for Peace Corps Korea, as well as some of the staff who were to train us. We were then put on buses that passed through farmland before entering the outskirts of Seoul.

Before long we passed the National Assembly and then drove over the Han River Bridge. From the traffic, the buildings under construction, and the layer of smog floating above us, we could see that Korea was far more developed than many of the countries a Peace Corps Volunteer (PCV) might have expected to be sent.

After a one-hour drive, our buses arrived at the Peace Corps office near the Gwanghwamun intersection.[1] We were then led to a nearby inn where we met a PCV who told us, "Okay, this is where you're going to stay. You've got to sleep on the floor." That was fine with me. What took me by surprise was hearing, "By the way, your luggage has been sent to the training facility in Cheongju, and you will be staying here for two nights." I could only think, "Gee, thanks, guys. That would have been nice to know." I had only packed enough clothes in my carry-on bag to last for the duration of our two-day flight, and we would soon discover that almost none of us could buy clothes off the rack that would fit. A glance around our rooms at the inn made it clear there were no bathing facilities there, so I wondered just how badly we would smell by the end of our stay in Seoul.

A PCV who was in town for the weekend came to greet us and gave us a tip on how to feed ourselves: "Most of the Chinese restaurants will have wax food in the windows so you can just point at what you want." It was past noon, so the volunteer went out to lunch with us and gave us an impromptu language lesson as he demonstrated how to order food. Learning the language seemed a bit hopeless at that point, at least for me. Whenever he answered the question "How do you say that?" I tried to listen, but it was difficult to hear what was being said and to catch all the nuances of the sounds. About the only word that stuck was "*yakki mandu*," so I ended up eating a lot of fried dumplings.

After lunch, we were left on our own in Seoul for the next day and a half. There weren't any activities planned for us, and we had no idea

---

[1] This is today called Sejong-daero Intersection.

what we were doing and had no one to guide us, so in small groups we started to venture out and explore the city. Seoul was busy, crowded, and, fairly dirty because of the layer of smog that hung over the city. Despite the smog and crowds, the mountains that surrounded the city gave it a certain charm. As well, many Korean people we met were friendly and went out of their way to help us, which made things easier. I spent much of the time walking around in awe, thinking, "Wow! We're in some place that's totally different. We have no idea what anybody is saying, but we'll figure this out." At least, that was how I felt. There were a few people in our group who never tried to make sense of things and left not long after we got there. But I looked at it as a new experience. We just had to take it as it came and assume that we'd figure a way through it all.

One thing we didn't get much of during our stay in Seoul was any understanding of Korean history or culture. No one from the Peace Corps pointed out landmarks or told us where anything was. They just said, "Don't get lost." We had no idea we were staying near two palaces, and instead headed toward Jongno and Myeong-dong. Since they had lots of places where we could become better acquainted over food and drinks, those neighborhoods suited the volunteers I had befriended just fine.

The group of volunteers I was training with was the 45th group of PCVs to be sent to Korea, known as "K-45." We had all first met in San Francisco several days earlier for an initial three-day training session at the California Hotel on Geary Street. Two PCVs who had returned to the United States on furlough after two years of service in Korea spoke to us and gave us a basic overview of what to expect. Otherwise, this session did not involve any language or cultural training. That was to come at the training facility in Cheongju, where these two PCVs would serve as our tuberculosis control instructors.

Our main task in San Francisco was to get vaccinated for diseases such as hepatitis, yellow fever, and encephalitis. Another important goal of this initial session was for the trainees to get to know each other and sort themselves into like-minded groups. After our vaccinations, we were all told, "You're not allowed to drink tonight," but a group of us promptly ignored this, perhaps showing the first inkling of a disobedient streak. Some of the people I befriended in San Francisco remained my friends throughout training, during our years of service in Korea, and even today. One person I befriended early on was Tim Warnberg. Tim was well-liked by the members of our K-45 group. Being tall, handsome, and athletic, the women all loved him, but the men really liked him, too. He was a nice guy, he wasn't pretentious, and he was a good person to have lengthy conversations with over a couple beers. He always had the most amazing stories to share. In fact, the Peace Corps hadn't flown him from his home in Minnesota to San Francisco—he'd hitchhiked. And he didn't go directly to San Francisco, either. We were all impressed as he told us his tale of making his way down to L.A., and then back up to San Francisco, because while hitchhiking, he was picked up by Mark Hamill—the main actor in the blockbuster movie *Star Wars* released the year before—and he had invited Tim to a party in Hollywood. I could only wonder how in the world he had managed to pull that off.

On the last night in San Francisco, we were all taken out to a Korean restaurant. It was not only the first time I'd eaten Korean food—it was also the first time I'd ever used chopsticks. It took me some time to figure out how to use them, so I didn't eat much. The next day we were taken to the airport, where we boarded a flight to Hawaii. We stopped only briefly in Honolulu, and from there, the flight to Tokyo was mostly empty except for our group of naïve Peace Corps trainees.

We had an overnight layover in Tokyo, where we stayed at a hotel near the Imperial Palace. We quickly learned who the more adventurous people in our group were. Most people said, "Oh we're just going to our rooms to sleep," and after eating at the hotel they went to bed. Tim,

Ron, Bohdan, and other members of our little group who had hung out together in San Francisco couldn't believe that. None of us had ever been to Tokyo, and we didn't really know anything about it, but we just figured, "We're some place totally new. Let's go wander around and explore."

At first, we wandered around in a bit of a daze because all of the signs were in Japanese, but after walking through some alleys, we stumbled upon a little family-owned restaurant. I don't think I'll ever forget the look of awe that crossed the faces of that family as their empty restaurant was invaded by six foreigners. From the way they stared at us the entire time, it seemed we were more entertaining than the TV. Though we spoke no Japanese and the family spoke no English, by miming and pointing we were able to get some beers and some food. We didn't know what we were eating—we were just pointing at things and saying, "Yep, let's go for it," and enjoying the novelty of it all.

Not every experience we had after our arrival in Seoul was as fun as that evening in Tokyo, of course. Returning to the inn after our first evening wandering around the city, I was left feeling depressed. Not only was it run down and located on a dingy side street, it was also a place where suit-clad businessmen came after drinking for short visits with women who were not their wives. A more positive experience, however, was discovering the traditional Korean bathhouse behind the Peace Corps office. Though my clothes may not have been clean, I could at least be confident that I was.

Cheongju

On Sunday, after two nights in Seoul, we were put on buses to Cheongju, the capital of North Chungcheong Province, where we were to receive our in-country training. The bus trip gave us the chance to see the

Korean countryside for the first time. The landscape was, as I wrote to my parents the next day, "very hilly but beautiful in its own way." I couldn't help but notice how bare the hills and mountains were. It seemed as if there were no trees anywhere other than those that stood in groups near villages or alone surrounded by rice paddies. Seeing people planting rice in the flooded paddies was another new experience—as was being told that one long stretch of highway could be converted into a landing strip should war break out.

Cheongju was a large city with lots of mountains off in the distance. After driving over some unpaved streets, we were taken directly to the Peace Corps Pre-Service Training Center, which was a two-story building that had been an inn before. Almost immediately after our arrival we were told by a staff member to follow them, so off we went. Before long we arrived at a high school where we saw a performance of traditional Korean music and dance. Having not had a chance to see anything like it in Seoul, I was so taken by it that I took out my camera and shot an entire roll of film.

After watching the performance, we returned to the training center where we were given the Korean names we were to use during our Peace Corps service. We were told that the Korean language instructors used our Christian names, as well as some background information about us, to decide on a Korean name that would be a good fit for us, either phonetically or in its meaning. The Korean teachers told us our names in Korean, showed us the Chinese characters, and explained their meaning. I was given the name Im Dae-oon (임대운 in Korean, or 林大雲 in Chinese characters) and was told the family name, Im, means "forest," and the given name, Dae-oon, means "big clouds." I liked this name. It was given to me by Im Dong-ook, or "Farmer Im," as he was nicknamed, an older gentleman who was one of our Korean teachers. From that point forward I was known by two names. To Koreans and some of my fellow PCVs I

28

was Im Dae-oon, to other PCVs and the Peace Corps I was still David. But from that day onward, for some reason, I identified more with Dae-oon than David.

With our new names in hand, we were introduced to the homestay families we would be staying with during our three-month training period. There was fierce competition in Cheongju to be a family that took in a Peace Corps trainee because it was very prestigious, and some families did this on a regular basis. One rule they had to follow was that they could not use the volunteers to teach their children English. After eating dinner with them at the training center, we followed them to our new homes. My host family lived above a store that the mother ran, while the father worked for the city. A grandmother also lived with them, as did two daughters and one son; another son was going to school in Seoul and sometimes came home on the weekends. The sons and one daughter spoke some English, so I was able to communicate with the family easily enough. The house had four rooms and a kitchen, and I was given a room to myself. I told them I didn't think that was fair, but they insisted.

Our Peace Corps training began the next morning. On entering the training center, there was a two-story atrium, where we had eaten the night before, which was sometimes used as a classroom or sitting room. Beyond that was a hallway with lots of small rooms. Some were offices for the administrators and teachers, and the rest were classrooms. There was a big board showing the class schedule. I started the day with a Korean class. In our language classes there was one teacher who taught six volunteers. The Korean teachers could all speak English but never did in class. Instead, they brought in colored sticks and used them to teach us colors and numbers before moving on to more complex sentences. Who would have thought that you could start to learn a language by using colored sticks?

There were also five PCVs who were there to train us in leprosy and tuberculosis control. These PCVs had already finished their two years of service and had stayed on to work as instructors. Most of us in K-45 were to be trained in tuberculosis control, so our classes related to this were held in the large room on the second floor of the building, while the six people focused on leprosy received their training in one of the smaller classrooms. In these theory-based classes we were taught how to read x-rays, stain slides, and do microscopy. We were also taught tuberculosis-related vocabulary and phrases in Korean that we would need to do our jobs. Though some of the English-language terms associated with tuberculosis control were new to me, I had studied biology and chemistry in university and so understood the science behind the disease and did not find these classes difficult.

Our classes started at 9 a.m. and finished around 5 p.m. or 6 p.m. After my first day of class I went home for dinner with my homestay family and then wrote my parents a letter. During my time in Korea, I wrote my parents once a week and sent occasional letters to my grandmother, my great aunt, and a few friends. Each letter was numbered to make sure that none had gone missing, which could occur due to censorship by the Korean government.

In that first letter, I gave the opinion that "I think I have grown twice as much in these 11 days as I have in the last 22 years." I wrote of Korea: "It is a very beautiful, proud country, making an American jealous that he is not equally as proud of his nation. This has made me open my eyes and for once I am getting my values straightened out." I also wrote that "The people are very emotional and show it, which is helping me to come out of my shell. Any apprehension I had is gone. I feel and know I shall like it here."

I enjoyed the classes that gave us a basic introduction to Korean culture, which were taught by our Korean teachers. This cultural training tended to be practical in order to help us understand what our role was going to be while working in a health center and how to function there with as little friction as possible. We were taught how to shake hands, how to support things with our left hand when passing them, and how to show respect when drinking in front of older people. While this was useful, I don't think these classes really did justice to the culture and history of Korea. It was in some ways glossed over, and I can't help but think that this was a missed opportunity, because they should have wanted us to become interested in the culture. I guess it was thought that our job was to work in the health center and not to take time off to go explore the country. In the end, if we wanted to learn about Korea's history and culture, we had to discover it on our own.

There was sometimes friction between me and my friends on the one hand and the Peace Corps staff on the other. We didn't always take some of the training activities seriously, such as when we were told during break time to practice speaking Korean and responded by saying things to each other in Korean such as, "Let's go down to the store and get something to drink." "Okay, let's do that." Perhaps because of this, about three weeks into our training some of the American staff decided we didn't respect Koreans or Korean culture and deemed us to be "culturally insensitive." The other staff followed suit. Considering that two of my "insensitive" friends married Koreans and either lived in Korea for years or returned often, while many of the "exemplary" volunteers have had little to do with Korea since their service finished, I can't help but think that the staff were wrong about us. They seemed to see our inability to fit the mold as being insensitive to Korean culture.

In Cheongju we mostly socialized among ourselves, but usually only on weekends. This was because we had long days of classes on weekdays and then usually went home to our host families for dinner. The American trainers tended to keep to themselves. As for the Korean staff, socializing with us for the women would not have been looked upon kindly, while the middle-aged staff would have found it awkward due to the age difference. On some of our free weekends we visited mountain temples and fortress ruins. We usually figured out how to find these places by asking our host families or getting directions from the Korean staff. The trips were always an adventure for me and my friends, but navigating was often a challenge because someone had to pay attention to where we were going by reading the signs. Reading was not one of our strengths at that time, however. Our language training focused on listening and speaking first and only began to introduce us to the alphabet later. This was done so we could at least have a basic grasp of how to read, but we were never really introduced to formal reading and writing.

To be honest, I never really made a connection with the language during our training. I had a difficult time expressing myself, in part because I've never been a big talker. Also, I was overthinking things and trying to speak sentences that were too complicated. Listening to Korean and understanding it came much more easily, however. A lot of our training focused on listening and repeating, which helped in that regard. I may not have been the worst student in our group, but I must have been close to the bottom. I did learn quite a bit of dining-related vocabulary, as well as Korean table manners, from my dinners with my host family, but it was only after I was living and working in the countryside and forced to communicate in Korean that I really connected with the language.

After three months of training, we returned to Seoul, where I affirmed my oath as a Peace Corps Volunteer on June 29, 1978. A few days before training ended, we found out where we were being assigned. I was assigned to the small town of Yeongam in Jeollanam-do, or South Jeolla Province, to work in the county health center as a tuberculosis caseworker. A few other volunteers were posted nearby as well. Tim was assigned to Kwangju, and Bohdan, who I had become good friends with during training, to Naju. After a farewell party, our newly minted group of volunteers headed out to our places of work throughout the country.

Affirming my oath as a volunteer was the final step in a process that had taken more than six months. Though I had thought of it as an option that would allow me to travel to faraway places and make a difference in the world, I don't exactly remember what made me decide to apply to the Peace Corps.

During my school years, which were spent in Westtown, in eastern Pennsylvania, I had ambled at a leisurely pace through school and life. I had enjoyed sports but never really applied myself as much as I could or should have. The same was true of my other interests: history, medicine, and science. I didn't know how to turn my enjoyments into my life's work, but then how could I when I didn't know who I was or who I wanted to be?

At West Chester State College, I initially decided to major in history, but my professors could never convey the same excitement that I got from reading history books, so after a year I switched my major to chemistry/biology, which was the closest major my school had to biochemistry. Though these courses were more interesting, I still didn't feel all that challenged. For the most part, college was something expected of me but that I did not know how to utilize to my advantage. Having to work nights to pay for my education and expenses didn't help matters. Something that did motivate me, however, was having my advisor tell me that I would never get into graduate school, let alone medical school, and should think about becoming, at best, a laboratory technician. I love to be challenged, especially by unequivocal statements with the words "never" or "can't."

Although I felt directionless as college ended, I was driven by a desire to make a positive difference, but there seemed to be no good tools to help me discover how to pursue that goal. I guess I made the decision to join the Peace Corps because I thought it could provide me with the opportunity to begin to find myself and do some good, something the recruiting materials suggested could be an outcome of the experience.

I started applying to the Peace Corps program in January 1978. Most of the process took place over the phone. Once I contacted the Peace Corps, I was assigned a representative who was to guide me through the application process and explain what positions were available. First, I had to pass an initial screening which included submitting letters of recommendation, an interview, and a physical exam. The letters and the short, face-to-face interview at the Peace Corps office in Philadelphia were no problem, but the physical exam proved a bit challenging.

The physical took place at a nearby Veterans Affairs Hospital. Being in excellent physical shape, I did not have any problems until the eye exam. I was first diagnosed with vision problems in the fourth grade, and the problem had worsened over time. The doctor was fascinated with my eyes and my slow progression toward poorer and poorer sight. In fact, he was so fascinated he came up with a diagnosis that was certain to remove me from the selection process and prevent me from joining the Peace Corps. He also mentioned that he wanted to examine me every three months for the rest of my life. Perhaps he saw publications and lucrative funding when he looked at my eyes. I contacted my Peace Corps representative, who told me that I could appeal the doctor's findings, and with some help from my regular ophthalmologist my application was put back on track.

Having passed my initial screening, my regional representative could now begin bidding on my behalf for the countries and positions in which I wanted to serve. These were limited, however, because most of the service opportunities the Peace Corps offered were for teaching English, which I had absolutely no interest in. I wanted my volunteer experience to revolve around my science education. The delay caused by my physical screening led me to miss opportunities in Nepal, Lesotho, and Grenada. Finally, one of the volunteer services that became available to bid on was for tuberculosis and Hansen's disease positions in south Korea. I chose this position but did not know if I would get it because of the archaic bidding process. Bidding started on one coast of the United States and then traveled from recruitment center to recruitment center until reaching the opposite coast. There was always the possibility that by the time your regional representative was called none of the positions you wanted would be available. My tense wait ended in early March 1978 when I found out I would be going to south Korea in April as a tuberculosis control worker.

Though I was finally in the Peace Corps, the country I was being sent to wasn't one I knew much about. All I really knew about Korea at that time was from the TV show *M*A*S*H*, and that my father had almost been deployed there in 1953 after he was drafted. I could barely find anything in the library about Korea and I had never heard much about it on the news.

Having lived with my parents while attending university, I had never really left home, or traveled on my own, or even flown in a plane before. I needed to get a passport and book a flight to San Francisco for the initial three-day training session. Getting the passport was easy enough because the Peace Corps arranged for all its volunteers to get passports that were tied to our Peace Corps status. They also booked the flight to San Francisco for me.

I had no idea what to bring, but correctly assumed hiking boots would be useful. My luggage consisted of two duffel bags, which my father told me was the best way to pack my things. I also slipped in the collected writings of Henry David Thoreau, whom I considered to be a kindred spirit. Something I knew not to bring was my shoulder-length hair and moustache, since I had heard they were not acceptable in Korea, so I made a local barber very happy as he cut off my hair and made me look presentable.

Finally, the big day arrived. My parents drove me to the airport, and we said our farewells at the gate. Before long I was aboard the TWA (Trans World Airlines) flight on my way to San Francisco. It was both an exciting and scary time as I set off, traveling on my own, intent on trying to make my way in life in a foreign country. I really had no idea what was in store for me.

In addition to the training sessions, there were also the evening bonding moments. David and three fellow trainees trying to sing a Doobie Brothers song acapella.

Trainees learn the classic Korean folk song *Arirang* from a Korean teacher during a class at the training center.

A cartoon from the Peace Corps K-45 training book humorously depicting one of the sticks used by Korean teachers during Korean-language classes. These were used because English was not spoken in these classes, which was challenging for David at first, but forced him to listen and observe carefully, something which has been a benefit ever since.

David in the early summer of 1978 during training.

38

Go where he will, the wise man is at home,
His hearth the earth, — his hall the azure dome;
Where his clear spirit leads him, there's his road,
By God's own light illumined and foreshowed

Emerson

There is an inward voice, that in the stream
Sends forth its spirit to the listening ear,
And in a calm content it floweth on
Like wisdom, welcome with its own respect;
Clear in its breast lie all these beneteous thoughts,
It doth receive the green and graceful trees
And the gray rocks smile in its peaceful arms.

Thoreau

In vain I look for change abroad
And can no difference find,
Till some new ray of peace uncalled,
Illumes my innermost mind.

Thoreau

성 · 명 : 임 대 운
생년월일 : 1956. 1. 1
출 신 주 : Pennsylvania 주
학 력 : W. Chester주립대학 생화
학
경 력 : 검사실 기사, 경비원
취 미 : 사진, 하이킹, 등산, 바이
올린

David L. Dolinger

January 1, 1956

Westtown School Westtwon Pa.
19395

West Chester St. ·College Biochemistry

Lab Tech.; Security guard;
Attendant for Mentally Handicapped
Emergency roomattendant
Photography, Sports, Hiking, Rock
climbing, Violin

– 6 –

David's page from the K-45 Peace Corps training book

39

Tim Warnberg during training in the spring of 1978. Tim was assigned to work as a Hansen's Disease co-worker at Chonnam University Hospital in Kwangju. Kwangju was his city, where he was a welcoming host to all PCVs.

Bohdan during training in the spring of 1978. Bohdan initially worked in Naju as a Tuberculosis Control worker. He later quit the Peace Corps, married a brilliant Korean artist, and moved to Waegwan to work as a teacher.

2. Settling in and Finding My Self

July 1978 to May 1980

B efore I could begin my service in Yeongam, I needed to get there, something we were all left to figure out on our own. Yeongam was more than a one-hour bus ride southwest of Kwangju. Halfway between Kwangju and Yeongam was Naju, where Bohdan was placed, so we traveled to Naju together. I continued onward for another half hour to Yeongam and stepped off the bus into the late afternoon sun.

Though Yeongam was the county's administrative center, which was the reason it had a health center, it was quite small and had no paved streets. There were only two Korean restaurants, several drinking establishments of various sorts, a few Chinese restaurants, a *dabang*, or tearoom, and a few places serving *twigim*, or batter-fried vegetables. I was soon to learn that the town had a single bathhouse that was only open in the winter.

I made my way to the health center, which was at the top of a small hill, and introduced myself to the office manager, Mr. Kim. The health center had arranged lodgings for me nearby, so I was taken there to drop off my bags. Then Mr. Kim, who was the only person at the health center who spoke some English, took me out for dinner with some other co-workers. Dinner included a live octopus that had been chopped up, and its still-wriggling tentacles were lightly covered in sesame oil and sesame seeds. Perhaps they were expecting me to say, "Oh no, never," but I decided it was fun and kind of cool, since I had never eaten something that could fight back. My chopstick skills while handling the tentacles and the fact that I enjoyed the food made a good impression on my new co-workers. Food challenges were often a part of my experience in Korea, but I always passed.

The next morning, I started work at 9 a.m. My first day was spent drinking tea and being introduced to the health center employees and county officials who worked in the building next door. That night I went back to my room for dinner. My room was in a *yeoinsuk*, a boarding house that rented out four rooms to people who worked in Yeongam during the week. It provided both breakfast and dinner, which was brought to my room on a small table. The rooms were in a compound which also housed the landlord's home on one side and a shared bathroom on the other. My room was ten feet[2] by ten feet with no furniture. There was just a mat, a blanket, a pillow, and a single light bulb dangling from a wire at the center of the ceiling. The ceiling was about six and a half feet[3] high, and the bulb hung at about five feet.[4] There was a traditional sliding paper door and a small window which looked out on a wall. The room, simple as it was, suited me just fine. It was paid for with

---

[2] Ten feet is about 3 meters.
[3] Six and a half feet is about 2 meters.
[4] Five feet is about 1.5 meters.

the stipend I received from the Peace Corps, which was small from an American perspective but like the salaries of our Korean co-workers. The stipends gave us the means to pay for food and lodging, and usually by the end of the month we were lucky to have anything left.

I didn't feel entirely ready for this adventure. I felt I lacked the language skills and didn't have a good understanding of what was expected. So, from the beginning, I observed, learned what was needed by my co-workers, and tried to help whenever I could without getting in the way. I spent my entire time at the health center learning, and those lessons have proven valuable to me throughout my life.

At the health center there were two people involved in tuberculosis control: my main co-worker and a lab technician who did all the microscopy for the smears to detect the bacterium that causes tuberculosis. There was also an x-ray technician and his assistant, two health center administrators, and four nurses. At first there was a doctor working there as well. He had just graduated from medical school and been assigned to Yeongam to fulfil his military service, but he told me over dinner one night that his father was going to have him transferred to Seoul. He left about two months later, and after that we never had a doctor on staff, so we were left to do everything ourselves.

What were the expectations of Peace Corps Volunteers working as tuberculosis case workers? This wasn't clear and differed from health center to health center. Some PCVs ended up teaching English to the county head and other officials, but luckily, I didn't have to do that. I did go to the girls' high school to speak to some of the English classes, but that only happened two or three times. From the start I also worked a half day on Saturday, even though I was told I didn't need to. I just thought that if my co-workers were doing it, I should too. I'll admit, however, that though my male co-workers had to share rotating night duty, which involved sleeping at the health center, I never did so myself.

The work I did at the health center involved screening individuals who had signs and symptoms consistent with tuberculosis. This entailed sending them next door for a chest x-ray, obtaining a sputum specimen, reading the x-ray, and staining and reading the sputum smear. The X-ray would tell you that there was a problem in the lungs, and then you would stain the sputum smear specifically for the organism that causes tuberculosis to see if they were putting the bacilli out into the air and actively spreading the disease. Depending on whether they were sputum positive for the bacilli or just had a chest x-ray that was consistent with tuberculosis, they would be placed on a regimen of up to three drugs for as long as two years.

I also went out with the community-based healthcare workers, who were the backbone of the tuberculosis control program in Korea. They worked for the health center but were assigned to a specific region in the countryside and lived in one of that area's villages. Their job was to go from village to village actively looking for people who had signs and symptoms of tuberculosis and to follow up with those who were receiving therapy. Their role was to be proactive and find people with illness and convince them to go to the health center, whereas the role of the health center workers was often reactive, to take action once they were visited by someone ill. There were occasionally health campaigns held during which the community-based healthcare workers and the health center worked together, but these were few and far between. When I went out into the field with the local health workers it was mostly to show people that the American was there and that he cared about their health and so should they. We were a marketing tool, but in some ways a reasonably effective one. I always enjoyed the experience. I got to take a bus down bumpy dirt roads and get off at a stop in the middle of nowhere and then walk to the first village of the day. These villages were made up of just a few houses, one of which would usually have a tiny store in it. After being introduced to the village head, we would ask him if anyone had tuberculosis symptoms. If so, we would visit them, obtain a sputum specimen, and ask them to visit the health center the next time they were in Yeongam. We also did follow-up visits to people being treated for tuberculosis. During these visits we had to count their pills to make sure that they were taking their medicine. They would usually take three different drugs, two of which were in pill form and one that was injectable. The pills were taken three times a day with meals. This was not an easy drug regimen to adhere to because the patients needed to take a handful of pills at each meal and the drugs could have unpleasant side effects.

It was on these outings that I really started to learn about the Korean people who were the heart of Jeollanam-do, and the heart of the country. On one bus trip out to the countryside, I was sitting next to a man in his 70s and we began to talk. Everyone always wanted to know where you were from, what big American city it was near, and why you were in Korea. It was the same with this old man, and I told him that I had grown up in the countryside. He asked to see my hands, which I showed him, and he immediately laughed and asked if that was true because my soft hands looked as if I had never worked a day in my life. He then showed me his hands, which were thick and calloused, and you could see the man's story in those hands. From him I learned to appreciate the hands of people when they came into the health center. I could see how hard people worked, and I learned that coming to the health center was a tough decision for some because they had to make a special trip to Yeongam and it meant a loss of earnings for the day. Things that I had taken for granted they had to think about and weigh their options.

* * *

I soon developed a routine. I would get up early, as I always have, and go out to walk and exercise a bit. The days when I went for a run brought stares. For people in Yeongam it was a new experience to see a young man, particularly a foreigner, running, though the older men and women who exercised in the park quickly got used to it. After exercising, I went back to my room, ate a small breakfast, and bathed. Since the only bathhouse in town was only open in the winter, I had to use an outdoor hand pump in the yard. In fact, there was never running water in any of the places I lived in Yeongam, only hand pumps. To bathe, I would go out in a pair of athletic shorts, fill up a big tub of water, dump it all over myself, soap up, and then repeat the process to rinse myself off. Later, when the weather began to cool, but before the bathhouse opened, I had to get up an hour earlier to warm up the water by using either the coal-fired stove used to heat the floor, or a kerosene stove I owned. Once the bathhouse was open, I would usually only go once or twice a week, but since I got there so early the soaking tub was sometimes not even full, so I didn't get the full benefits of the bathhouse other than running hot water.

Once I had bathed, I would arrive at the health center by 9 a.m. when work started, and stay there until at least 5 p.m. Once work was finished, I would sometimes go out with my co-workers. I probably went out with the nurses as often as I went out with the men. What was fun about going out with the nurses was that they all acted like my older sisters, as they all were trying to take care of me. We would go to a little store with plastic tables and chairs outside and have a beer with some fried *jwipo*, or filefish, or maybe some squid, and would sit and chat. These outings usually took place during the warmer months when we could sit outside the store since it would have been considered improper for the nurses to go to a drinking house. When I went out with the nurses they all had to go home by 6:30 p.m., so everybody would leave and I would have the rest of the evening to myself.

When I went out with my male co-workers, it was different. We would go to a *suljip*, or drinking house, which was often a tiny place with a couple of tables. Sometimes they had dirt floors, but the food was fantastic, and there we would usually drink either *soju* or *makgeolli* rather than beer. I preferred *makgeolli*, the farmer's drink that was usually homebrewed from rice. Though using rice to make alcohol was illegal, this was ignored in the countryside, and in my county almost all of it was homebrewed. As a result, you could get it almost anywhere, even in the smallest village, and they all had their own unique flavor.

My co-workers would sometimes challenge me by trying to find the spiciest food they could, or would offer me food such as *hongeo*, a kind of skate that is fermented in a way that results in an overpowering smell of ammonia. Unlike the after-work gatherings with the nurses, with the men I was out for the evening, until about 10 p.m. or 11 p.m. At that time everyone had to leave to get home, or at least find some place to stay before the midnight curfew, so usually people tried to down as many drinks as they could, which was not really something I liked to do.

In addition to the drinking houses where I went with my co-workers, the town also had two *gisaeng* houses where men could go to drink with *gisaeng*, or *hanbok* clad hostesses. These women were usually young and would serve them, sing for them, and potentially do more. Since these establishments were usually very expensive, they were someplace you would only go to finalize business or impress clients. As it turned out, however, I became quite familiar with one of the *gisaeng* houses because the madam, or owner, had a son who was then a junior at a high school in Kwangju, and she wanted him to improve his English. Every time he came home, one of the women would come looking for me and say, "The young master is here. Would you mind coming and helping him with his English?" So, I would go to the *gisaeng* house and they would give us a room to ourselves where we could talk. The boy, who was a very nice young man, spoke English well due in part to his own enthusiasm, but also because his mother had put a lot of money into his education and wanted him to escape from the situation she had been in. She had started working in a *gisaeng* house when she was very young and had luckily been able to save enough money to open her own and run it as the madam.

What made the experience more interesting was that the women, if they weren't working, would come in and sit with us and feed us. As a result, I became friends with some of the women who worked there and would greet them when I saw them on the street or at the health center. This led some of my Korean co-workers to ask in a judgmental manner how I knew them. When I explained my English-teaching arrangement, they reacted with surprise, and then became obviously jealous when I added, "And they feed me beer and food all night until I leave."

Another group of women I interacted with were the young women who worked at the only *dabang*, or tearoom, in town. By ordering a single, expensive cup of instant coffee, you could sit for hours in a comfortable chair and have a conversation, or just sit and read. I had first discovered tearooms in Cheongju during our training, but I hadn't grown accustomed to spending time in them until I started spending more time with Bohdan. After we first arrived at our health centers, I met Bohdan in Naju or Kwangju two or three times a month. We had different preferences, as I liked to be outdoors in the mountains or countryside, whereas Bohdan enjoyed the city and tearooms. It was really Bohdan who taught me how to relax in a tearoom for hours on end.

When I visited the tearoom in Yeongam, it was always fascinating to observe the interactions there. Coffee was served by younger women who in most cases provided other services, particularly when they made "coffee deliveries" to men who were usually looking for a mistress. The women working there were curious about me as a foreigner, and they liked the fact that, unlike some of the other customers, I didn't try to pinch or grab them, so when they had nothing to do they would come over and talk to me. Since I seemed interested in only talking to them, and didn't speak *banmal*, or "talk down" to them using informal speech, they decided I was harmless. It was fun to talk with them, and it was a good way to expand my Korean vocabulary, as well as my understanding of the politics of Yeongam. I had interesting discussions with them and with the tearoom owner, with whom I would use honorifics because she was older than me. She probably thought I was a clueless foreigner who didn't understand where we all were in the social strata, which wasn't the case. These interactions led to me having several "older sisters," which is the only way I can explain the friendships I developed with these women. They took care of me when I visited, sometimes getting me the best seat near the TV when I went in to watch a sports match.

The other draw of the tearoom, other than these conversations and the sports events on TV, was the air conditioning. In Yeongam it was the only place with air conditioning. I had a fan in my room, but due to the danger of suffocation that Koreans believed fans posed, the fans had limitations. One was that there was no on/off button, just a timer. The fan would turn off after a maximum of two hours. Luckily, my father had taught me well, so I knew how to rewire the fan to bypass the timer. I was told many times to turn my fan off at night, however, and sometimes at the first place I lived the owners would come in while I was sleeping and turn it off for me. As a result, I would wake up at 2 a.m. in the stifling heat and wonder how in the world the room had gotten so hot.

After a few months I decided I wanted to live someplace where I could cook my own meals. I moved into a house built in a modern *hanok* style that was divided down the middle. The owner, a widow in her 70s, lived on one side in a single room and I lived on the other. Behind my room was my own kitchen, which I was able to equip with help from Tim. When Tim first moved to Kwangju he had taken over the room of another PCV who was leaving, but after a few months he decided to move in with a family. As a result, he had no need for the kitchenware or the kerosene stove the other PCV had left behind, so he kindly gave them to me.

As a result of the move, I became much more familiar with the market and the people working there. Since I could make my own food, I would stop by the marketplace to get what I wanted to eat that day. Sometimes I would talk to the women working in the market and would look at something and ask, "Okay, what can I do with this?" Once they realized I was trying to cook for myself, they said, "Oh, you're the son I wish I had," and gave me all the recipes I wanted. With their help, I learned to make my own *nakji-bokkeum*, or octopus stir fry, as well as simple things such as stews made with bean paste or kimchi.

As I became more familiar with Yeongam, I also began to frequent the *twigim* shops. *Twigim*, or batter-dipped and oil-fried vegetables, became a go-to comfort food for me, as it was for elementary school students. The *twigim* shops in Yeongam were clustered together on a road near the elementary school. They were usually run by young mothers in their late twenties or early thirties and consisted of one room in the front of a house with a dirt floor and some chairs. For the children, the most important thing was that they had Korean *manhwa*, or comic books, to read. When I visited, I would sit around with a group of elementary school students and eat *twigim* and thumb through the comic books. I enjoyed the visits because the owners were nice, the comics provided a good way to pick up some vocabulary, and I could stay there for a couple of hours without spending much money.

Kwangju

It was normal for a lot of Peace Corps Volunteers in Jeollanam-do to go to Kwangju, then the provincial capital, on the weekends to meet up, drink, and then head home on Sunday evening. I didn't do a lot of that. I was the oddball because I didn't really feel a strong need to speak English and meet Americans every weekend. There wasn't a lot that I missed from home, other than my family, but we wrote each other letters every week. I was more interested in exploring where I was living.

When I did go to Kwangju, which was perhaps once every month or two, the PCVs from Suncheon, Mokpo, and other places in the region who came into town would meet up with each other. There were times when an informal phone chain was organized to pass along information about the date and time people would be there. I would get a call at my health center from Bohdan in Naju, and then I would call people in Mokpo and they would call others. In Kwangju we usually stayed at one of the *yeogwan*, or small inns, near the Provincial Capital, and there we would leave notes letting each other know where we were.

Whenever we met up in Kwangju we always wanted to meet Tim, who was based in the city. This was partly because he was a great guy who was fun to spend time with and who was always up for a drink. Also, Tim's Korean language skills were the best of the entire group, and his vocabulary was enormous compared to the rest of us, so he had discovered a lot about the city. When we visited, he always knew great places to go. He introduced us to Japanese restaurants where we could spend the equivalent of $4.00 on a 20-ounce[5] beer, and they would cover the table with plates of seafood such as shrimp and king crab legs. It was like heaven for someone who usually had to budget so carefully.

Bill and Kathy, a couple based in Mokpo, also knew places for us to go. They introduced us to the tents and carts that appeared in the streets after the sun went down, and some of the more exotic foods we tried,

---

[5] 20 ounces is about 600 milliliters.

such as grilled sparrows, which you ate bones and all, were enjoyed with them.

On occasion I went to Kwangju by myself to explore the city. I discovered a small alley not far from the Provincial Capital building that I liked to visit because there were several places that served *pajeon*, or scallion pancakes, though my favorite was *bindaetteok*, or mung bean pancakes. These places were essentially a shack with a small covered front where the women cooked, in front of which were outdoor stools and tables for customers. The owners lived in the building behind where they cooked and served food. I liked to sit and observe while eating pancakes and drinking *makgeolli*. I was initially considered an oddball because these places tended to be frequented by people who were less well off, but after a few visits they accepted me. Every time I went, I chose a different place to eat at to avoid showing favoritism, which the women appreciated.

When I met up with other PCVs in Kwangju, we would often head to a tearoom to have coffee and talk. Kwangju had lots of tearooms and they were usually easier places to sit and talk than bars, especially since you could just buy a cup of coffee, expensive as it was, and sit there for hours. Of course, if you sat too long in a tearoom in Kwangju, inevitably someone would come over and say, "Excuse me, may I practice my English with you?" For me, I could never say no. When I went by myself to Kwangju, I would often talk with students who approached me this way, and eventually made friends with several of them. I also met a few through Tim, and most of the students he knew were a little more outspoken and more liberal in their political views than other students I spoke with.

Quite often when they found out I could speak Korean, their desire to practice English would fall by the wayside and we would start to speak in Korean. Once that happened, they would only revert to English when they wanted to talk about things like politics, and then only in whispers, because you never knew who was listening. When it came to politics, they would usually ask what my opinion was of the Korean government. Though I would start by saying, "I'm not really supposed to talk about politics," and "This is your country," I would eventually offer my opinion of their government, but I would also give them my opinion of my own government as well. They were curious about what I thought about democracy, but never talked about socialism or communism. They weren't interested in that, at least from the conversations I had. These discussions usually focused on human rights, democracy, and wealth redistribution. They wanted to make things better for the less well-off and prevent the rich from getting too rich. Though they started these conversations because they were interested in my opinion, it was through these interactions with my Korean friends that my interest in Korean politics and human rights issues began to grow.

Not every interaction in Kwangju was as pleasant as those. One hot and humid summer day when I was walking through an alleyway near the express bus terminal on my way downtown, I passed a group of young men who were sitting outside drinking, talking, and laughing. One of them, who had obviously not noticed my longish hair, which I had deliberately grown out to avoid such confrontations, cursed at me in Korean for being an American soldier. He asserted that I probably took advantage of Korean women and didn't care about their culture. I decided to say something, so I whipped around, and told him in the best Korean I could muster that I was not a soldier, that I worked at a health center helping tuberculosis patients, and that I actually knew quite a bit about Korean history. They stopped and stared at me with their mouths agape for a moment before apologizing profusely and offering me a shot of *soju*. I told them it was okay, and that it was fine to be displeased with U.S. soldiers being here but asked them to remember that not all foreigners were soldiers and that some of us loved and enjoyed Korea.

In-service training and trips to Seoul

Twice a year Peace Corps Volunteers had to attend in-service training sessions. These were usually between three and five days long and took place near Seoul, and were attended by the rest of our K-45 group and sometimes other groups as well. Whether we were working with tuberculosis or Hansen's Disease, we would talk about our experiences, suggest how we could improve, and learn what people were doing to have more impact. The experiences of the other PCVs in our group were very diverse and differed for each volunteer.

To be honest, I don't know that I got a lot out of these sessions. They were nice because they allowed us to meet with friends we hadn't seen in a while and have some fun. At one session in Suwon, however, we were chastised for making paper airplanes and throwing them out the windows of our inn, which upset the staff. Despite the fact that children on the street below clearly enjoyed trying to catch the airplanes, which led to us teaching them how to fold them, we were once again deemed to be culturally insensitive. To me this highlighted how the Peace Corps staff seemed to think that "proper decorum" was more important than fostering cultural exchange.

Another opportunity for PCVs to meet was provided by the Embassy or the military when they hosted Thanksgiving and Christmas dinners for us and other Americans. During my first year, I went to the Thanksgiving dinner hosted by the Embassy and held at Yongsan Garrison, but it was the only time I attended. To me, Seoul wasn't really a place I wanted to go. I only went two or three times a year, either for my yearly physical or while passing through on my way to someplace else. It was a long trip to get there, either by taking an overnight train or spending most of a day on a bus, and it meant having to take time off from work. I also didn't really have a desire to seek out other Americans, and never understood the mentality of those volunteers who wanted to sneak into Yongsan Garrison to go to the McDonalds, the movie theater, or the cafeteria.

Another draw for volunteers in Seoul was the Friday night gathering held at the Marine barracks in Compound 2, next to Gyeongbok Palace, which housed the Marines who guarded the Embassy. I attended this twice, and, like most PCVs on a budget, was happy to take advantage of the free food and alcohol the Marines provided to any Americans who showed up. Even today I'm thankful the Marines did this for us, and the Marines I met there were really good people. But I also had some discouraging conversations when I visited. After a few drinks you could get the U.S. Embassy staff to talk very honestly, and it was there I was told by one Embassy staff member, "We don't care about anything that goes on here other than protecting U.S. business interests and making sure U.S. companies working here don't have any problems." It was disheartening to realize that human rights were not as important to the Carter Administration as its public statements suggested. I was quite taken aback, because I, like many Americans, had believed President Carter's focus on human rights might actually make a difference in the world.

For this and other reasons, I wasn't very interested in going to Seoul when I was a PCV. I was much keener to explore and learn about Yeongam and Jeollanam-do, which had become my new home.

I got to know Yeongam well as I explored the county on foot. I loved the outdoors and enjoyed hiking along the coast or going into the mountains and discovering temples and talking with the monks. I was lucky because Wolchulsan, or "rising moon mountain," is a short walk south of Yeongam and I spent a lot of my free time there hiking, free climbing, and exploring. The first weekend that I was in Yeongam, I was taken up the mountain by the sons of the owner of the boarding house where I was rooming. After that I went on my own and followed the existing trails or even made my own.

It was a beautiful place. I liked to go up the mountain early in the morning and hike until it started to get dark. Sometimes I would just go up, find a nice spot by a creek, put my feet in the water and just relax there for the day. On other trips I would free climb the beautiful rock formations and take in the views from the top.

* * *

This desire to explore the outdoors, and to do so by myself, grew out of my experiences as a child. Before the age of seven I grew up in London Grove, Pennsylvania, which was about 31 miles[6] southwest of Philadelphia. It was a very rural area, one that served as a playground for my brother and me since we had all of the surrounding farm fields to play in. We also explored the grounds of the nearby New Bolton Center, part of the University of Pennsylvania's veterinary school, where my mother worked as a laboratory technician.

I attended a Quaker kindergarten at the London Grove Friends Meeting, and then was enrolled at Unionville Elementary School. When I was in the first grade, I had my tonsils removed over the Easter break. This was a standard procedure for children in the 1960s, and once it was finished, I seemed fine. While recovering at home, however, it became clear something was wrong when I started having trouble breathing. My mother and father rushed me to our family doctor, who told my parents to get me to the hospital as quickly as possible. Once we arrived, I was taken to the children's ward where I soon fell asleep. When I woke up, lights

---

[6]   31 miles is about 50 kilometers.

were glaring down at me and I was surrounded by people with masks on, including a nurse with Asian features. I could feel them doing something to my neck, but it wasn't painful. I quickly passed out again.

It was only when I was leaving to begin my Peace Corps service that I learned the full story of what happened that night. In a note my mother gave me, she wrote, "We nearly lost David that night—in fact his breathing and heart did stop but thanks to skill and quick action and most importantly prayer he did live." I had stopped breathing after my throat had swollen shut, so the doctors had to perform an emergency tracheotomy to help resuscitate me. I awoke, unable to speak, with a metal tube in my throat. After being in the hospital for three weeks, I was confined indoors until the new school year started five months later and was not allowed to meet friends, which likely contributed to my inability to fit easily into social situations and my preference for solitude. As well, due to the lack of oxygen, I have had to deal with issues such as difficulty with reading out loud and my ever-worsening eyesight. But surviving that experience also taught me that no matter how difficult a task might be, I can always push myself to accomplish it.

Another formative experience was being educated at Westtown Friends School, an exclusive private Quaker school. When I was seven, we moved to Westtown and settled into a house located on campus. My father maintained the school's boilers and worked as a handyman. Because he was an employee, I was able to attend the school and receive an education that my parents would not have been able to afford otherwise. The students at the school came from varied backgrounds: children of the rich or well-off Quakers, students on scholarships who usually came from places such as inner-city Philadelphia, and staff and faculty brats like me. It was a very diverse community, but one with high expectations for the students to make something of themselves.

The education I received both in school and as part of the Quaker community had a great influence on the shaping of my ideals, my spirit, and my path. I was taught to stand up in a nonviolent manner when I saw injustice. I was also instilled with a sense of community and unity that looked beyond who people were, where they came from, or what they looked like, and I was taught to respect the community and the individuals within it regardless of different points of views. At school we studied different religions, we had to do chores around the campus, and we had to attend meetings for worship twice a week. Due to my medical emergency in the first grade, I likely had a different perspective compared to most students since I tended to observe rather than worry about friendships and socializing.

* * *

Though my trips up Wolchusan were usually by myself, the paths meandered past temples where I could talk to the monks. A small shrine on a trail I liked to hike was manned by a single Buddhist monk, with whom I would visit and have discussions on a variety of topics. He was the first person to tell me that he thought that my Korean name was a good one and implied that it would have an impact upon my life. Sometimes I updated him on contemporary affairs, but usually he imparted his understanding of the human spirit, his beliefs in Buddhism, and his thoughts on the beauty of nature, while I listened and asked questions. Through these conversations I gained a greater understanding of Buddhist teachings, and found that they complimented what I had been taught during my Quaker upbringing. Rather than accepting either in an uncritical, religious manner, I tried to learn from the teachings of each and use the parts that felt right for me as a philosophical guide to how to live my life.

My trips to the rural townships to check on tuberculosis patients also brought me face to face with attitudes toward life and death that were different from my own. On one occasion I visited a family that had three generations living in close contact. The grandfather had active tuberculosis and was infectious, but stopped taking his drugs because of the side effects. I tried for 10 to 15 minutes to get him to take his drugs, but he refused. It didn't matter what logical argument I made; he just said, "No." He finally looked at me and said, "I am over 70 years old. I have lived a good life, but I am now tired and don't want to take my medicine. I am done! I just want to finish my life's journey." I later talked with his son and he said it was all right; they would watch their health, and I should just accept that the grandfather had made up his mind and had made peace with his decision. Because he could no longer work in the fields and contribute to the family's wellbeing, the grandfather saw himself as imposing upon his son's family, and he thought it best to stop burdening them. This mindset was something I had never encountered before, but the belief that individuals should sacrifice themselves for the betterment of a larger whole was something I would confront in a dramatic way during my final weeks as a Peace Corps Volunteer.

As my time in Yeongam went by, I began to feel like I was accepted as part of the community. When I first arrived, children would often point at me and draw attention to my foreignness by yelling "*Miguk! Miguk!*" This gradually changed, however. I knew I had been accepted when people would see me and show little reaction, as if to say, "Oh, it's just you."

One reason for this was that I tried not to be treated differently. At that time, county workers and sometimes even high school students were mobilized in the spring to help the farmers plant rice, and in the fall to help with the harvest. During my first fall in Yeongam, my co-workers at the health center tried to convince me that I didn't need to take part in this, but I wasn't willing to be given a pass. While some of the people from the other county offices would be expected to work for a few days, because I was American and we were from the health center, we would usually only go out for a day. For the harvest we were given a scythe and had to bend down, grab handfuls of rice, cut it, lay it down, and keep moving along. In the spring we were knee deep in the water transplanting the rice seedlings. It was something I developed a strong affinity for, and whenever I see rice growing, I remember it fondly.

* * *

While I was rather content with my life in Yeongam, the political situation in Korea at this time was gradually unravelling. I did not have a deep understanding of Korean politics, but my student friends kept me informed about what was happening. In October 1979, student demonstrations in Busan and Masan were suppressed by the military after martial law was declared. Some students I knew made comparisons between these events and the student revolution of 1960 that had overthrown Korea's authoritarian first president, Syngman Rhee. They wondered if the demonstrations could bring about the end of Park Chung-hee's 18-year-long dictatorship, but Park's assassination took us all by surprise.

I knew something was up as I walked to the health center for my half-day of work on Saturday, October 27. I noticed that the flag was at half-mast and there was a lot of whispering going on. When I walked in, I was immediately told the news that President Park was dead and was given a black ribbon to wear on my left shirt pocket. On the day of Park's funeral, all of the workers in the county offices met in the courtyard to listen to the live radio broadcast. In the immediate aftermath of Park's death there was much uncertainty. No one knew how the transition of power was going to proceed. Would a new dictator from the military step in, or would there be a transition to democracy? Throughout the fall, my friends and co-workers appeared to be spending more time watching and listening to the news to see what would happen.

Then, six weeks later, the December 12 incident, known as "12.12," occurred. Major General Chun Doo-hwan, who was investigating Park's assassination, carried out a coup within the army and replaced its top leadership. The news about 12.12 depressed my student friends and led my co-workers and other acquaintances to acknowledge that it was probably going to be the same old "normal" with a different dictator. Because Chun did not take immediate charge of the government, however, people weren't sure what to think, and neither was I, though his appointment as acting head of the KCIA in mid-April seemed to confirm he was reaching for power. In response to this, by mid-May, students in Kwangju were holding pro-democracy rallies off campus, just as students were in Seoul. My student friends felt that a combination of demonstrating, letting their voices be heard, and pressure from the Carter government could still lead to democracy.

In 1979 I got the chance to meet a well-known critic of the government. I was told by another PCV about the weekly Quaker meeting in Seoul that was held in the home of Ham Seok-heon, who lived near Ewha Womans University, and decided to attend. Ham was a remarkable figure. Born in 1901, he took part in the March First Independence Movement against Japanese colonial rule in 1919, became a Quaker, and was imprisoned at various points in his life for speaking out against authoritarian rule, be it by the Japanese, the Soviets (in northern Korea), Syngman Rhee, or Park Chung-hee. He was present at multiple Sunday meetings that I attended during my time in Korea. The meetings were an hour long, as Quaker meetings typically are, and we all sat on the floor in a circle along the outside wall of a large room. There were occasionally other foreigners there, such as Quakers from the United States, Maryknoll

61

Fathers, and laypeople. There was also a simple communal lunch after the meeting which helped to bring the Quaker community together.

In the spring of 1980, I was also preparing to extend my Peace Corps service for a year. Most PCVs didn't, but I enjoyed being in Korea and wanted to see what interesting opportunities might arise. Setting up my next placement took some time, but I eventually learned that I would be working at the Ministry of Health's tuberculosis laboratory in Seoul. At an interview there in the spring of 1980, I met the doctor overseeing the lab. We discussed the research they were doing to develop urine tests that would determine whether people receiving treatment were taking their drugs or not, and I was excited by the opportunity to work on such projects. Though PCVs who extended were allowed a month-long furlough in the United States, I had little interest in this and wanted to get started as quickly as possible.

I didn't really visit Kwangju much in early 1980. This was partly due to being busy with the extension process, and partly because a number of the PCVs I knew in Jeollanam-do had ended their service early. Bohdan, for example, had been dating a woman in Seoul, but when they got married in 1979, he decided he didn't want to subject her to life in small-town Naju, so he quit the Peace Corps and found a job teaching on the U.S. base in Waegwan, near Daegu. After that, I went to Kwangju by myself. If I wanted to meet Tim, I knew where he lived and he knew where I stayed when I went to Kwangju, so it wasn't hard to find each other. When I received an invitation to attend the wedding of an English-teaching PCV scheduled for May 17, I decided to take that Saturday off and spend some time in Kwangju for the first time in over a month.

The rooftops of Yeongam, taken from the fourth room I rented, in 1979.

A day out in Wolchulsan and Dogap-sa with my fellow Health Center co-workers.

The rear courtyard of the second room I rented, with traditional jars with the hand pump I used for drinking water and bathing.

Climbing in Wolchulsan with PCV trainees.

'My Mountain,' Wolchulsan.

On top of the world, overlooking Yeongam from Wolchulsan.

Part II

The Kwangju Uprising, May 1980

3. Hope Amid Tension

Friday, May 16 to Saturday, May 17

Friday, May 16

On Friday, May 16, after I finished work, I caught a bus to Kwangju, where I planned to spend the night before heading to the wedding on Saturday morning. On the way to Kwangju, the bus stopped in Naju, where Miss Park, a nurse from Naju Health Center, got on. I had met her while visiting Bohdan in Naju, and even after he left, I had seen her occasionally on the bus to or from Kwangju. Miss Park was very outgoing, and because we knew each other and hadn't seen each other for a while, she came and sat with me. Though it was usually awkward for a Korean woman to be seen with a foreigner, she didn't seem to care.

She was going to Kwangju for the weekend to spend time with her brother, who was a third-year student at Chonnam University. She inquired about Bohdan and we talked about my tuberculosis work during the 45-minute ride to the Kwangju bus terminal. Neither of us had eaten dinner yet, so we decided to grab a quick bite to eat. She then invited me to come meet her brother.

Her brother lived between the railway station and the campus in a second-floor room he shared with another student. When we arrived, he was having an intense discussion with three other students about how activism should proceed after recent events. Several days of demonstrations in Seoul had peaked the previous day with a march by tens of thousands of students, but students there had called off future demonstrations at the behest of the government, which said the democratization process could only resume once the students returned to classes.

Miss Park's brother and his friends were obviously very knowledgeable about what was happening. They told me they had been taking part in demonstrations throughout the spring. I did not ask them directly, but based upon the amount of detailed information that they had about events in Kwangju and the rest of the country, I assumed their involvement went beyond merely participating in demonstrations.

One topic of discussion was whether the government and Chun Doo-hwan could be trusted. They also specifically asked me what I thought the U.S. government would do, and if I thought the Carter administration was supporting Chun Doo-hwan. Since Peace Corps Volunteers were not supposed to participate in politics, I tried not to get too involved and told them that they needed to do what they thought was right. I did add, however, that I thought it was their right to protest for democracy.

To be honest, I felt out of my depth when I was asked these questions. I didn't feel I knew enough about Korean politics to offer any meaningful answers. Though I had learned a lot from my conversations with students in Kwangju over the past two years, I still felt my political knowledge was naïve at best. It was difficult to learn much because most of the people I knew had government jobs, so they were always very careful about what they said and never discussed politics. Taxi drivers could be great sources of information about what was really going on in Korea, but they weren't always the easiest people to talk to because they would shut down the conversation if you were too inquisitive. Many people also believed that some PCVs were feeding information to the U.S. government, which made people reluctant to speak to us on these topics.

Remembering the conversations that I'd had at the Marines' TGIF event at the U.S. Embassy compound in Seoul, and concerned that the students might place too much hope in the United States, I cautioned them that, despite U.S. government rhetoric about human rights, it was more concerned about the stability of Korea insofar as it benefited the interests of U.S. companies.

During our conversation, the students told me that there was to be a torchlight march that evening from the train station to the Provincial Capital building. Then, like the students in the rest of the country, they were going to halt the demonstrations and see how the government responded. They said they had to leave to prepare for the march. As we parted ways, I decided to attend as well and told them I hoped to see them later. I quickly dropped my bag off at an inn and walked to the train station. People were gathering at the square in front of the station in preparation for the march. It was peaceful and stood in contrast to the demonstrations I had seen before in Seoul. There were no riot police, only officers in normal uniform directing traffic away from the protesters.

I followed the march from the sidewalk, because even though I was concerned about Korea's future, I did not think it was my place to march with the students due to my status as a Peace Corps Volunteer. Several people, both citizens and students, approached me and started conversations because they wanted to make sure I understood what was happening. People I talked to seemed hopeful that this would urge the government to act and ensure that democracy would take hold. The citizens I spoke to thought the path toward democracy would open because students had come to their senses and were willing to go back to classes and let constitutional processes move forward. The students I talked to were perhaps not as hopeful, but they had concluded that by starting and then stopping the demonstrations they could influence the democratization process.

The march ended with students holding their torches aloft at the fountain in front of the Provincial Capital. I had hoped to run into Miss Park and her brother, but luck was not on my side that night. As the students dispersed, I headed to the inn to get some sleep.

Students gather around the fountain in Kwangju during the peaceful torchlight protest on May 16, 1980.

Saturday, May 17

I awoke early the next morning and walked to the bus terminal to take a bus to the wedding, which was about an hour's ride southeast of Kwangju. I arrived around 10 a.m. and met up with the other PCVs who were attending the wedding. The groom was a K-46 English teacher I'd gotten to know, and the wedding was being held in the bride's hometown. The other guests were English teachers from Jeollabuk-do (North Jeolla Province), along with a few who were based in Korea's southeast.

The wedding was the first I had attended in Korea, and was a beautiful, traditional ceremony held in a park in the early afternoon. The bride and groom both wore *hanbok*, bowed a great deal, and exchanged sips of rice wine. After the wedding, there was a reception of sorts at the bride's home, and we spent the day enjoying ourselves. In the early evening we headed to a drinking house close to our inns.

Much like whenever PCVs got together, there was a fair amount of drinking, talking, and discussion. It was interesting to compare our experiences, as I was in a very rural area, while the other PCVs were teaching English in larger towns or cities. Only a few of us discussed the political situation in Korea. Some of the others had been in Seoul at the end of October when President Park was assassinated, while others had been there on December 12 when Chun Doo-hwan staged his coup within the army. Unfortunately, they brought little to the discussion other than the experience of having been there, but it was a perspective I didn't have. In Yeongam we had no tanks deployed and no gun shots, just the black ribbons we all wore after the assassination, and just whispers concerning the events of December 12.

We ate, drank, and talked until around 9 p.m., when we all headed to our inn. Some of the PCVs had to get up early to catch buses home.

4. "We cannot let them treat us this way!"
Sunday, May 18

I awoke to the news that martial law had been extended throughout the country. I met a few of the other PCVs and we went out for breakfast and discussed what was happening. At first, we thought it wasn't too big a deal, perhaps just a response to all of the recent demonstrations. Then we started to hear some details that were disconcerting. Kim Dae-jung and other opposition leaders had been arrested, and a meeting of student leaders in Seoul had been raided and students arrested. Considering that the students had decided to end their demonstrations, it seemed like an extreme response. We discussed what all of this might mean. The consensus was that this was the final act of a coup d'état by Chun Doo-hwan. After eating breakfast, I went for a walk and talked with two other PCVs, and then just after noon we went to a drinking house and continued the discussion.

After a few hours I decided to head home. I caught a bus to Kwangju and arrived in town sometime after 5:30 p.m. As we pulled into the bus terminal, I smelled tear gas in the air. After two years in Korea, it was a familiar smell, and not one that I associated with good things. In the terminal it was more crowded than usual, and I could feel the tension. I learned that people were trying to get tickets because the buses were set to stop running earlier than usual. I tried to get a bus back to Yeongam, which I could normally take until 9 p.m., but I was told, without any explanation, that there would be no more buses leaving until the next day, which meant I would have to spend the night in Kwangju. I also learned that a curfew was going to be announced. I bought a ticket for the earliest bus the next morning and started to walk toward the part of town where I normally stayed, near the Provincial Capital.

The walk there was very eerie, as there weren't many people or cars on the street. Before long I saw military trucks parked in the side streets and groups of armed soldiers. I assumed there had been a demonstration, but seeing soldiers, rather than riot police, was something new. Unlike the aftermath of protests I had seen in Seoul, where people had continued going about their business, the atmosphere in Kwangju felt very different. The people I saw had their heads down and seemed intent on avoiding the soldiers and getting out of the street as quickly as possible.

As I was walking down Geumnam-ro, the main street heading to the Provincial Capital, I saw Tim. I was surprised to see him because I had never run into any other PCVs while walking in Kwangju before. Tim was visibly very upset. As we walked toward the Provincial Capital building together, he described the things he had witnessed that day and pointed out where they had taken place.

As he later described it in his own writing, he had been downtown in the morning when a small group of students started demonstrating, calling for the end of martial law and the release of Kim Dae-jung. Combat police challenged them, meeting the students' stones with tear gas, which engulfed not only the students, but also passersby and families out enjoying their Sunday morning.

Although this was not too different from demonstrations in Seoul, soldiers arrived downtown in the middle of the afternoon and began beating with truncheons any young men they came across, and chased the fleeing crowds into the surrounding alleys. Tim described to me how he and another PCV fled into a store with a dozen other people to get away from the troops, but soldiers burst into the store and started clubbing everyone. One soldier was about to hit Tim when he realized with surprise that Tim was a foreigner, so he turned around and left. Tim also saw troops deliberately go into other stores and shops to pull out young men. He told me that once he realized that the troops were hesitant to do anything when he was around, or to hit him, he began putting his arms around people being beaten, which caused the soldiers to stop and target someone else instead. In this way, he was able to use the fact he was a foreigner to protect a few of the young men.

It was hard to believe what he was telling me. It just became more and more surreal as he described what had happened, particularly the indiscriminate beating of anyone who was young, regardless of whether they were participating in the demonstration or not. His description of events seemed to be confirmed by the uneasy atmosphere downtown, however. As we walked down Geumnam-ro, almost every other side street had small groups of soldiers with gas masks at their side. Some were obviously armed. Occasionally we encountered small groups of people huddled together in the side streets. From their clothes and the way they stood together and kept watch, we suspected they were plain-clothes government agents, perhaps police or KCIA[7]. Unlike these people, groups of normal citizens would usually disperse and walk away when they saw

---

[7] Korean Central Intelligence Agency

us coming, perhaps afraid that they might be detained for speaking to foreigners.

This wasn't true of everyone, however. Tim took me to a construction site near the Provincial Capital building to show me where students had armed themselves with rocks. As he was describing and pointing out the movements of the students and the troops, we noticed a man walking purposefully toward us. He was likely in his 70s, had white hair and a white beard, and looked very distinguished in his light blue *hanbok*. He was walking as quickly as he could, clearly intent on speaking with us.

Once he reached us, he immediately began speaking to us in Korean, assuming we would understand.

"Do you know what happened here today?" the gentleman asked, breathlessly.

"Yes, grandfather. I saw what happened," Tim answered.

"Did you see it also?" the gentleman asked, looking at me.

"No grandfather. I just arrived in Kwangju," I replied.

He then looked at us both and said, "The soldiers beat innocent people, people who were not involved in the protests. The soldiers went after the young, even going into stores to get them!"

"What else do you know about what happened?" Tim asked him.

"They were not regular troops. They were black berets," he replied. "What they have done is wrong! They should not go after innocent people who were not even involved! We cannot let them treat us this way! The citizens of Kwangju should defend themselves and fight back!"

He then turned and went on his way. Tim and I looked at each other in amazement. We then began to discuss what might happen next, and we wondered whether or not it was over. We both hoped it was, but after talking with the elderly man, we couldn't be sure. We tried to figure out why the troops had been so brutal. Tim speculated that people must have died, as he had seen bloodied, unconscious citizens being dragged in the streets by soldiers and thrown into the back of military trucks. This was something that neither he nor I had experienced before, so we were truly at a loss to understand what was happening.

As the 9 p.m. curfew approached, Tim invited me to his place, which was near the train station. Tim lived with a family—a middle-aged mother and her son, Sun-jae, who was in his early twenties. As we approached the house, Tim asked me not to talk about what was happening in front of the mother, as she was worried about her son. They lived on the second floor in a living space with two bedrooms, a kitchen, and a living room. The communal bathroom, where we could wash up, was downstairs on the ground floor.

When we arrived, Sun-jae's mother was making dinner and Sun-jae was in the room he shared with Tim. We sat down to eat, though I didn't have much because I had lost my appetite. The tension in the house was obvious, and when we retired to Tim and Sun-jae's room after eating, Sun-jae told us his mother had asked him not to leave the house, so he had not been outdoors all day. Tim only shared some of what he had seen with Sun-jae because he was afraid his roommate would want to get involved. We talked for about two hours before going to bed.

5. Whispers and Whirlwinds

Monday May 19 to Tuesday May 20

Monday, May 19

I needed to get back to Yeongam to be at work at the health center by 9 a.m., so I woke up early to catch the first bus. When I said goodbye to Tim, we both assumed that what had happened yesterday was over. During the ten- or fifteen-minute walk to the bus station, I couldn't sense any of the tension of the previous day. I didn't see any troops in the city, nor during the bus trip to Yeongam. This made me think that nothing more was going to happen. I was supposed to pass through Kwangju again on Wednesday to go to Chuncheon, northeast of Seoul, for in-service Peace Corps training, so I figured I would be able to find out more then.

Once I arrived in Yeongam, I walked home, washed up, and headed to work. At the health center there were some discussions about what had happened in Kwangju on Sunday, but people focused initially more on the expansion of martial law and the arrest of Kim Dae-jung and other opposition leaders. The consensus was that Chun had now solidified his power and would be the next dictator.

These conversations were whispered, because people really didn't know who to trust at that time. The KCIA had informants everywhere, and they may have even included the people I was treating for tuberculosis. Whispering and being careful about who you talked to were just healthy habits that everyone had at the time. Fear of the potential consequences, such as losing one's job and being blacklisted, worked to keep people quiet.

Much like any other day, people being treating for tuberculosis stopped in to get their medications. In the afternoon some of these people, mostly middle-aged men and women who had gone to Kwangju earlier in the day, told us that the violence that had occurred Sunday was continuing. In fact, they said it was getting worse and becoming even more indiscriminate. It was even possible that deaths had occurred. Based on what they had seen and heard, they warned that young people should stay off of the streets because the troops were grabbing young men for no reason. Some quietly told stories indicating that the troops were being just as violent to young women if they thought they were involved in the protests.

As the day went on, we heard more stories of the troops' brutality, and some of those returning from Kwangju told us that the troops there were not regular martial law troops, but "black beret" paratroopers, corroborating what the older gentleman had told me and Tim on Sunday. This news brought confusion to the hushed conversations. Why would paratroopers be used for riot control? The students had said that they would stop protesting and return to classes, but after martial law was expanded, they were denied access to the campus, which made no sense. What was going on? Why was the government's reaction to the demonstrations so brutal? Why was this happening, and why was it so different from past demonstrations?

The more stories we heard, particularly about the presence of the black berets and the indiscriminate nature of the violence against young people, the more worried my co-workers became. Many had family in Kwangju, and they were frightened for their safety. The phone was busy all afternoon as people called their loved ones in the city to make sure that they were okay. We tried to keep working as we normally did and covered for people who were busy making phone calls. As the hours passed, I grew increasingly concerned. This kind of violence was not normal for Korea. I worried about the people I knew in Kwangju, particularly the students. But this couldn't go on, I thought. Koreans wouldn't kill Koreans, would they?

One thing that reassured me somewhat was that there had been no word from Peace Corps headquarters to tell us what we should be doing. Perhaps things weren't as bad as we were hearing because the Peace Corps would tell us if it wasn't safe, wouldn't they?

After work I went home, made a light dinner, and read for a while before going to bed.

What I didn't know was that while I had been leaving Kwangju that morning, the military had rushed more paratroopers into the city, and as a result the clashes had become even more violent. Tim, in fact, was a front-line eyewitness and, just like the day before, he had gotten directly involved, intervening to prevent people from being dragged away by the troops and helping to carry injured people to a medical clinic, but it would be a few days before he told me these stories.

Tuesday, May 20

At the health center the next day there was more whispering. We weren't as busy as we had been on Monday, which was a good thing since it wasn't easy to focus on work. My co-workers were having a harder time getting in touch with their loved ones and friends in Kwangju. People were still coming into the health center and bringing news from Kwangju, but not as often as the day before. The stories they told, and the descriptions of the soldiers' brutality were much worse than on Monday. We even heard rumors that the soldiers had shot people to death or killed them with bayonets. Anyone who wasn't worried the previous day certainly was by this point.

Tearooms had TVs, so some of my co-workers left to go get coffee and to watch the news, which was certainly not something they normally did. The news didn't really shed any light on the situation, however, and there was some quiet discussion about the fact that the news reports didn't match what we were hearing about the situation in Kwangju. We tried to sort rumor from fact. From what we had heard about the indiscriminate nature of the black berets' violence, gunfire, and even deaths, no one seemed safe, particularly young people. What was happening and why? There was dread in the air. People kept hearing that the violence against Kwangju's citizens was escalating, and they had no idea how or when it was going to end.

I was supposed to attend a Peace Corps in-service training session in Chuncheon on Wednesday. That night, over drinks with some co-workers, I told them I was still planning to go. I had heard nothing from the Peace Corps regarding the training session or the situation in Kwangju. My co-workers tried to talk me out of it. They were worried about me having to pass through Kwangju to get there, though that was precisely why I wanted to go. I was worried about Tim and the students I knew in Kwangju, so I made up my mind to return to the city to see if they were okay and to confirm for myself what was happening.

6. The Path Forward
Wednesday, May 21

I woke up on Wednesday, the Buddha's Birthday holiday, certain that passing through Kwangju was a good reason to try to attend the training session. If it turned out that everything in Kwangu was all right, Tim and I could go to the training session together. I didn't really think about what I would do if things weren't all right.

When I got to the small bus station in Yeongam, I found out from others waiting for the bus that all phone service to Kwangju had been cut off since the previous night. This, along with knowing that the violence was increasing in Kwangju, made me feel even more concerned, and made it imperative that I get to Kwangju. By this point it was clear that I wouldn't be going to Chuncheon. I was able to catch the first bus at 6:30 a.m., but when it reached Naju, the bus driver told us he wasn't going to go any farther. I walked up to the bus driver and asked him why. He said that because of what was happening in Kwangju he would go no farther and that if I was smart, I wouldn't go to Kwangju either.

I ignored his advice and decided to continue on my way. Something kept telling me to go to Kwangju. I didn't know why I felt this way, but I knew I had to get there. The problem was that it took 30 or 40 minutes to drive there, and I wasn't sure how to proceed. I approached some taxi drivers and asked them how much it would cost, but they wanted up to 50,000 won ($100 back then) for the trip. There was no way I could afford that on my Peace Corps salary.

Having taken the bus to Kwangju many times, I was familiar with the route. I was young and athletic, and I had packed light, carrying just a daypack and my camera. I decided to walk. I optimistically figured it would take a couple of hours, but in fact it took much, much longer than that. Luckily, it was a beautiful day for a walk. There were only a few clouds in the sky and, wearing a T-shirt as I was, the temperature was quite comfortable. After walking for a while, I approached a point on the highway to Kwangju where a long, straight stretch of the road had been widened so it could be used as an emergency landing strip in the event of war. As I was walking along this section of the road, an oncoming truck and bus caught my eye. The two-ton military truck had people standing in the back, while the bus had people leaning their upper bodies or heads out of the windows. Both the truck and bus had banners hanging on their sides. It suddenly dawned on me that the vehicles had been commandeered by protesters. Astonished by what I was seeing, I pulled out my camera and took a photo as the vehicles, preceded by a taxi, approached me.

I watched as they passed and headed toward Naju. The banners read "Kim Dae-jung must be freed" and "Chun Doo-hwan must resign." The passengers were mostly young men, and they were all singing and shouting. I waved to them as they passed, and they cheered. They were taking the word to people in southern Jeollanam-do that the citizens of Kwangju were fighting back and standing up for democracy. I felt elated as the vehicles drove by. Perhaps this would turn out to be a democratic spring after all.

Taking that photo had immediate consequences, however. After the truck and bus passed me, the taxi that had preceded them quickly did a U-turn and headed directly at me. It swerved at the last moment and stopped about four feet[8] away from me. Whereas the driver was dressed in regular clothes, a man in the back seat was dressed in camouflage military fatigues with riot gear. The man in military fatigues confronted me. Speaking rapidly and forcefully in Korean, he demanded I give him my camera. I quickly and calmly replied in Korean, "No."

The man then stuck his head and arms out the back window and tried to grab my camera, but I was standing out of his reach. He again demanded I give him the camera. I refused to be intimidated, and standing my ground, I calmly refused and said that he had no right to take my camera. This was repeated a few more times until the driver intervened. Speaking clearly in English with an American accent, he told me the passenger was a KCIA agent and that all he wanted was the film. I told the driver in Korean, no, and that if they were KCIA agents, I needed to see both of their national ID cards, because I wanted to record their names, addresses and citizen numbers. The soldier ducked back inside the taxi for a moment before abruptly leaning out the window and thrusting a long, heavy, square-edged stick of wood at my chest. I saw it coming but didn't move and just stared at his face, which was contorted in rage. I slowly looked down and saw that the end of the stick was half an inch from my sternum. I still didn't move but I felt my insides loosen. I once again demanded their ID cards. The man then yelled at the driver to follow the bus and truck, and they sped off.

As they left, a middle-aged woman who had been walking down the

---

8 Four feet is about 1.2 meters.

Protesters in a commandeered truck and bus on the road from Naju to Kwangju. In the taxi in the foreground was the KCIA agent who confronted me.

road toward me stopped and spoke to me. She had clearly heard the conversation and said that I should have just given them the camera, that they might have hurt me had I kept arguing. I told her that I could not just give them the camera or film, that it was important to capture what was happening. Just like any mother, she begged me to promise that next time I would just give them what they wanted, because next time they might hurt or kill me. She told me that she had children my age who lived in Kwangju, but she had not heard from them since Tuesday morning. Though she said they were good children who would not join the demonstrations, she was worried because the increasing brutality and indiscriminate nature of the violence meant that no one was safe from the soldiers. I told her not to worry, that I, and her children, would be okay, and we both continued our separate ways.

Deciding that I didn't want to meet the two men in the taxi again, especially out in the countryside where there might be no one to witness the encounter, I left the main road and set off across the fields. I knew the area well enough to not worry about getting lost. Once I had walked far enough to be out of sight of the road, I decided that a check of my underwear was in order. I was glad to discover that the man who had rammed that piece of wood at me had not literally scared the crap out of me.

As I cut across the rice paddies and fields, I didn't see anyone else. The only exception was when I passed through a small village where a traditional farmers' dance was being held and life seemed to be continuing as normal. People were a little shocked at first to see a foreigner, but with a quick hello in Korean, they relaxed. Hours passed as I walked, though I wasn't really paying attention to the time.

Once I neared the city limits, I returned to the main road. I couldn't see any soldiers, and the only vehicles around were the trucks, jeeps and buses being driven by citizens who were trying to spread the news of the soldiers' brutality, and of the citizens' desire to stand up to them.

Soon a large, two-ton military truck returning to the city slowed down and stopped next to me. A group of young men in an upbeat mood were riding in the back. The driver asked me in perfect English if I would like a ride into town. We were both curious about each other and spoke for a few minutes. I explained who I was; he was an English professor at Chonnam University. He declared that he and the men in the back had decided to take action not for themselves but for their children and future generations of Koreans. Talking to them made me realize that I might have a role to play as a witness to what was happening in Kwangju. I turned down his offer of a ride because I felt that I had to walk into the city.

Once I was inside the city limits, I saw someone who looked familiar walking toward me. Once she was close enough, I realized it was Miss Park, the nurse from Naju Health Center who I had run into the previous Friday. We couldn't believe we were meeting each other again. I was surprised that she was just now leaving the city, while she was surprised that I was returning.

She began to explain to me what had happened over the past few days. She spoke of the increasing violence and described how, in response to this brutality, the taxi drivers had joined the protests the previous evening by driving in a large group down Geumnam-ro, and that finally the citizens of Kwangju had driven the martial law troops out of most of the city and back to the Provincial Capital building. I could hardly believe it. I was amazed to hear that regular citizens had joined the students. At that time in Korea the average citizen never got involved in student demonstrations. It was expected for students to act as the conscience of the nation and to take part in demonstrations, but upon graduating and obtaining a job, all of that changed for most of them. The average working person was worried about their life, about providing for their families, but the soldiers' indiscriminate violence had hit a common nerve and changed all of that. This was something new and, at least during the time I had spent in Korea, unheard of.

Miss Park explained that her brother and his friends had been participating in the demonstrations, but were all right. Wanting to stay out of harm's way, she had decided to walk back to Naju since it would be safer there. After talking with me for a few minutes, she changed her mind, turned around, and headed back into the city with me. As we approached the city center, we could feel an atmosphere of joy among the citizens. It showed in their faces and in the way they acted.

We occasionally saw jeeps with young men in them who were trying to recruit other young men to join the protests. We also occasionally passed by the burned-out shells of taxis and other vehicles. As we neared Geumnam-ro, we saw a parked jeep with a young man standing in the back using a bullhorn to address the people gathered there. As we got nearer, I saw an unforgettable sight: lying on the hood of the jeep was a man in his early 20s who had been brutally beaten to death. I had never seen anything like it before. I was saddened to think that someone could do something like that to a fellow human being. Miss Park told me she had seen this man's body before, and others as well, but had no idea how many people had died because many bodies had been taken away by the military. I was to find out later that a number of bodies that had been similarly beaten and bayoneted were being carried to different areas of Kwangju by groups of young men who wanted to speak to the people and to provide evidence of the military's brutality.

Being a foreigner, I stood out, and people were curious why I was there. After the young man finished his appeal to the people, he stepped down from the jeep and came over to me while other people prodded me toward him. I greeted him in Korean and he asked me who I was and why I was in Kwangju. He was a little disappointed that I was not a reporter but was happy that I spoke Korean as it made communicating easier. He pointed to the body and explained that this was what was happening to Kwangju's citizens, that it wasn't right and that the citizens needed to protect themselves from the soldiers who had declared war on Kwangju. He, like many people to come, wanted me to bear witness and to make sure the U.S. government and the world learned what was happening to the citizens of Kwangju and understood that they were not going to stand for it any longer.

In fact, many people stopped and talked with me to explain what they had seen, heard, or experienced. What they had in common was that they all believed the citizens had to fight back, and that the course the citizens were following was the correct one. I could feel that the citizens of Kwangju had become united in their fight against oppression and brutality.

After the young man left, we continued toward the city center. As we got closer to Geumnam-ro, I could hear an occasional gun shot. I had never been around guns before, and though it was not a sound I liked hearing, I didn't flinch. I wanted to find out what was happening, and I assumed that no one was firing at me, which, in retrospect, was not a very smart assumption.

Suddenly, I heard a helicopter followed by gunfire. I stopped walking and was looking up at the sky when a helicopter came into view. I saw a man dressed in camouflage fatigues aiming a gun out of the open side of the helicopter. He appeared to be shooting down toward Geumnam-ro. I then heard shouting and noticed that the street was empty. Miss Park grabbed me and pushed me toward the open door of a store. When I stuck my head out the door to see what was happening, Miss Park grabbed me and pulled me back in, saying, "Are you crazy? The military has been flying over Geumnam-ro and shooting at people!" She then explained that they were targeting groups of people, even in the side streets. It was then that I realized that white skin and round eyes were not much protection when this kind of terror was being rained down from the skies. Several people around me cursed under their breath at the military. Everyone was obviously scared and thought that I was a bit simple for not immediately running for cover.

After the sound of the helicopter receded, we continued walking toward downtown. To get safely to the other side of Geumnam-ro, we used a pedestrian underpass. There Miss Park and I parted ways. She was going back to her brother's place, and I was going to see if Tim was home. After two fortuitous meetings during a turbulent time, we said goodbye, and that was the last time I ever saw her. I still don't know what happened to Miss Park, but I pray that she and her brother stayed safe and have lived long and fruitful lives.

I saw citizens in the side streets next to Geumnam-ro but didn't stop to see what was happening because I was focused on getting to Tim's to make sure he was okay. When I got to his place, his homestay mother told me he had left the city for work but was supposed to return that day, though she wasn't sure when he would get home. I decided to go see what was happening downtown and headed back toward Geumnam-ro.

Most of the people I saw on the way were young men in their 20s and 30s, and perhaps a few high schoolers; there weren't that many women. For every block I walked there was a different group of people gathered, and each group seemed to have a leader. Once again, I attracted attention since I was a foreigner, so I was approached by various people who wanted to explain to me what was happening.

I eventually decided to walk down a side street branching off of Geumnam-ro that was full of people. I noticed that none of them were attempting to walk out onto Geumnam-ro or trying to see what was happening. I poked my head out from behind a building to look down the street and saw armed soldiers, tanks, and personnel carriers in front of the Provincial Capital building, which was about four blocks away. I was suddenly jerked backward by one of the people standing in the side street who said, "You have to be careful! The soldiers are trying to pick off anyone who shows their face!"

This made it clear just how dangerous the situation was and drove home the fact that the soldiers were actually trying to kill people. While I stood there, I heard the soldiers firing randomly down Geumnam-ro. It seemed ridiculous that they were firing at heads that poked out, or were firing at random, and I wondered what they were trying to accomplish. Looking back, it seems they were trying hard to either keep citizens from gathering on Geumnam-ro, or, since citizens were staying out of sight, were trying to incite a response from the citizens.

To be sure, the soldiers' actions had provoked a response, and it was around this time that I first noticed a number of citizens carrying guns. It was then that I realized just how desperate the citizens must have been to resort to arming themselves. Still, their weapons all looked like antiquated rifles compared to the M-16s the soldiers were using. When I asked about them, I was told that they were M-1 carbines that likely dated from the Korean War[9]. I asked one of the armed students where

---

[9]   Korean war began on June 25, 1950, and ended with an armistice on July 27, 1953.

he had gotten his gun, and he told me there had been raids on police stations and armories. I learned later that citizens had been sent to the countryside and neighboring towns to seize more weapons, including mining explosives. The people that I talked to spoke only of using them in self-defense. I didn't see any citizens use their weapons against the soldiers that afternoon. In fact, the people I spoke with explained that they did not want bloodshed. They hadn't wanted it to come to this, but citizens were being gunned down, so they had no choice but to defend themselves. I started to worry that there could be a bloodbath, because I couldn't see how a dictatorship would allow its citizens to take up arms against it without taking retribution.

After speaking with people, I decided to go back to Tim's to see if he had returned home. As I was walking along the main street that runs in front of the train station, I saw Tim walking with Judi Chamberlin, another PCV who was based in the city but who I didn't know well. Tim and I were both happy to see each other and started speaking at the same time, asking each other if we were okay. They had also walked into the city, but from the north, where they had seen lots of troops. Talking all the while about everything we had seen, we walked to Tim's and dropped off our bags. Tim's place was to become our headquarters for the remainder of our time in Kwangju.

We then went for a walk toward the center of the city and approached Geumnam-ro from a side street about five blocks from the Provincial Capital. I started to take pictures of people in the side street, including those who occasionally peered around the corner of the building, when a man in his late 20s or early 30s angrily yelled at me to stop taking pictures. I lowered the camera and we asked him why, and he explained that the government had been known to analyze photos from newspapers and journalists to track down protesters. This, he told us, was how a number of protesters in Busan and Masan had been identified in the fall of 1979 and subsequently detained. I told him that I wouldn't take pictures of people, but I wanted to get pictures of Geumnam-ro and the Provincial Capital buildings. He confirmed once again that the soldiers were shooting at anything that appeared from around the corners of the buildings. We made sure that he understood we were concerned PCVs, not journalists, which finally seemed to satisfy him.

We decided to find a side street closer to the Provincial Capital building, and it was there that we saw another foreigner. Tim had met him before, and introduced him as Donald Kirk, a journalist who wrote for the *Boston Globe* and the *Christian Science Monitor*. We talked with him about what we had seen. He asked us if we knew what was happening elsewhere in Kwangju and the surrounding towns and cities. I described how I had gotten into the city, and his interest was piqued by my description of the trucks and buses I had seen headed toward Naju.

There were several medical clinics in the side streets along Geumnam-ro. They were small so they usually didn't have the ability to keep people overnight. We decided to check and see if they were treating wounded people and found them full of patients with injuries ranging from gunshot and bayonet wounds to blunt force trauma. Many of the wounded were not college-aged at all, but rather men over the age of 30, the kind of people who worked hard to make ends meet. This fact, along with the injuries and wounds they had suffered, made it clear to us that citizens of all ages were standing up together against the military's indiscriminate violence. It was inspiring to see, but also incredibly sad that it took the murder of so many innocent people to make it happen.

The staff at the clinics were surprised to see us, but they were so busy that we didn't explain who we were, only that we were interested in understanding what was happening. Everyone was too busy to talk for long, and most conversations occurred as they went about their work. For all of the staff, it had been a terrible and hectic day. The doctors in some cases were overwhelmed by it all. They were busy trying to find and contact patients' families and trying to transfer people to larger hospitals. We were told of three deaths, one each in three of the five clinics we visited.

By the time we finished visiting the clinics the sun was beginning to set. Though there was no one to enforce the curfew, we decided it would be a good idea to get home before it got dark. We walked back to Tim's house, which was a 15-minute walk from the city center.

After we returned home, Sun-jae's mother made a nice dinner of soup, rice, and side dishes for us. We turned on the news but were left mystified by the reports about rioting and looting in Kwangju. They did not match at all what we had seen or heard from others. The mood was very somber. Was the truth of what was happening even getting out of the city? Sun-jae and his mother tried to lighten the atmosphere by turning the TV to a historical drama, but it was hard to concentrate on the show with everything that was racing through our heads.

Sun-jae's mother was overly protective of him, and of us as well, so we never talked about what was happening in front of her. We retreated to Tim and Sun-jae's room to whisper about the things we had seen while always trying to keep emotion out of our voices. This was difficult because we were all so confused, upset, and unable to understand why any of this was happening. It also didn't help that our conversation was occasionally punctuated with the sound of gunfire coming from the direction of the Provincial Capital building.

Tim and Judi talked about their walk back into the city. Coming from the direction of the nearby ROK / US air force base, they had seen the main road into Kwangju lined with waiting soldiers, Armored Personnel Carriers (APCs) and tanks. While discussing some of the rumors floating around, Tim told us he had heard that people had been fired on and killed by a machine gun the military had set up at the bus station. When

I shared details of my experiences that day, I never told the others about my confrontation on the road from Naju. I thought it was potentially too frightening because we had always believed that, as Americans, we were impervious and untouchable. My encounter that day suggested otherwise. I was also still trying to get my head around not only that incident, but everything else I had seen and been told. What did it all mean? What was really going on?

Though we were anxious because we didn't know what the next morning would bring, we knew that we needed sleep and eventually decided to go to bed. I found a place on the floor in Tim and Sun-jae's room, while Judi left to go sleep in Sun-jae's mother's room. It was some time before I finally drifted off.

7. Liberation at What Cost?

Thursday, May 22

I woke up fairly early, but not as early as Sun-jae's mother, who had already gone to the market to do some shopping. From not only the downstairs neighbors, but also people at the market, she had heard that the troops had pulled out during the night. Over breakfast we discussed this incredible news, but had so many questions. Was it over? How bad had it been? Who was in charge now? After breakfast we decided to go downtown to find out what was going on. Sun-jae's mother told us to be careful, though she knew that as Americans we would be safer than her son, who was not allowed out of the house.

As Tim, Judi, and I walked downtown, there was a sense that the city had awoken that morning with renewed hope. The troops were gone! There was an air of excitement as we encountered people. They were friendly, always saying hello, asking us if we had eaten, and asking who we were. Many wondered if we had heard that the troops had withdrawn.

We passed by several people of various ages who were working together to clean up their neighborhood. We saw them removing debris such as rocks and shoes and sprinkling water to keep the dust down. Closer to downtown there was more extensive damage such as burned-out buses and cars and battered roll-down metal storefronts, one of which appeared to have been smashed in by a vehicle.

As we walked down Geumnam-ro, we could see that the area in front of the Provincial Capital buildings, normally a busy traffic roundabout with a large fountain at its center, was full of people milling about. It looked considerably different from the previous day when the troops controlled the area. In the absence of the troops, it was now a central square where citizens gathered. Most of them were working-age men, but there were also many young, university-aged women present. High school students, mostly boys, stood out in their school uniforms. Although the square was not jam-packed with people, it was crowded enough that we had to pay attention as we weaved through the crowd. People were gathered more tightly in front of the gates of the Provincial Capital, where we could see people coming in and out of the compound. Some were being turned away at a newly established security checkpoint. It was manned by armed young men, some of whom were wearing riot police helmets. It appeared that they were only letting in people who had some sort of pass.

Just like us, people had come there because they wanted to find out what was going on. Many were sitting on the ground as they waited to hear news about who was in control, who had been killed, where the bodies were, and whether the soldiers were coming back. The people around us were curious who we were, and once they learned that we spoke Korean, they were eager to speak with us. Many of them hoped we would share what was happening with the outside world. By talking with them, we were able to find out that the city government was nowhere to be found, and that a citizens' settlement committee, initially made up of mostly older civic and religious leaders, had been formed to negotiate with the military. We also learned that both the military and the citizen's militia had set up barricades on the outskirts of the city, which would make it difficult to enter or leave Kwangju.

The process of cleaning up the city accelerated later in the morning as groups of people were organized by the citizens' committee in a large, concerted effort to remove not only the broken glass and debris but also the burned-out and wrecked cars, trucks, and buses from Geumnam-ro.

Amid this bustle we were approached by two journalists from England and Denmark who spoke no Korean and were without interpreters. When they found out that we knew the city and could speak Korean, they asked if we could interpret for them. Tim decided it would be a good idea to take them to Kwangju Christian Hospital and to Chonnam University Hospital, where he worked. That morning it still wasn't clear how many people had been killed or injured, so by going to the hospitals we could try to figure this out and make sure that the reporters got that information. Tim also hoped that at the Kwangju Christian Hospital there might be a missionary or English-speaking doctor we could talk with to get a better idea of what was happening. The reporters would also be able to talk directly with them.

We went first to Kwangju Christian Hospital, where we found the hallways crowded with beds because the wards and ER rooms were full. The morgue was similarly full to overflowing, and there were numerous people there looking for missing family members.

Just like the previous evening, we saw people with gunshot wounds, bayonet wounds, and blunt force trauma from being beaten. Seeing such injuries, I couldn't help but wonder how someone could do such things to another person. It was unbelievable. Having only seen violence in movies and news broadcasts from Vietnam during the war, these injuries seemed unreal, like something out of a horror movie.

We asked the doctors how many victims had come into the ER in the last 24 hours, but they were unable to give an answer. All they knew was that they had never been that busy before. They hadn't received any emergency cases that morning, so the doctors had time to talk. In fact, when they realized we spoke Korean and had reporters with us, they approached us and were eager to share what information they had. The doctors answered our questions, described the kinds of wounds they had seen, and showed us X-rays.

One X-ray we were shown was that of a young man who had reportedly been shot from a helicopter. We could see that the bullet had entered the left shoulder, traveled downward, and exited just above the young man's right hip. The doctor also showed us evidence, in the form of an X-ray, that some people had been shot with non-standard bullets. The doctor knew from his military training the types of wound to expect from a "normal" bullet. The X-ray he showed us did not have a clean entry and exit path, and, because the bullet flattened on impact, the internal damage was extensive. The bullet also broke into fragments, which were visible in the X-ray. These were expanding bullets, which are used to inflict as much damage as possible. These bullets had been outlawed for use in war since the Hague Convention at the beginning of the 20th century but could still be used for internal policing. The military had used bullets which by international law could not be used against north Korea.

The doctors were not the only people eager to talk. Everywhere we went, people wanted to talk to the foreigners, because they wanted their story to be heard. People visiting the hospital were also very cooperative and wanted to get information to the reporters. Even those searching for their children or mourning over their loved ones' bodies wanted to talk. Because the women were often overwhelmed by their grief, it was mainly the men who did the talking.

Some of the stories the parents told us hit me hard. Trying to hold back their tears but failing, grieving fathers told us how their children had died. Some told us that their children had not been demonstrating but had been walking to work or home when they were attacked for no reason. They were at a loss to understand why their child had died in such a seemingly meaningless way. Others told us how their loved ones had been pulled off buses by soldiers who beat them unconscious and left them to die. Why had the paratroopers been so brutal? Knowing that the students had called off their demonstrations and planned to return to classes, the violence made no sense to the parents. In some cases, the fathers vented their anger at the government, and a few even argued that violence and resistance should continue because their child had died.

We then walked over to Chonnam University Hospital. Once again, there were more injured, more people wanting to talk to us, and more dead. The morgue was overwhelmed, so most of the sheet-covered bodies were lying on rice-straw mats on the ground outside the morgue. We counted 27 bodies. Some had already been identified and their families were present, but others had not. No one knew who they were, but they were treated with dignity as they awaited identification.

Since we were with journalists, I think people assumed that I was one too until I spoke with them in Korean. In our conversations, it became clear that people wanted the journalists and other foreigners to get the truth out. They knew the news media in Korea was not telling the truth about what was happening in Kwangju. I was told that this was why the two TV stations in the city had been burned down. I decided it would be a good idea to record what was happening in the morgue. Because of my conversations the previous day, I asked permission before taking photos.

As we stood among the bodies, the only sound I could hear was the crying of family members as they sat with their loved ones. Wandering among the bodies were those who were looking for loved ones they had lost contact with during the preceding days and still had not heard from.

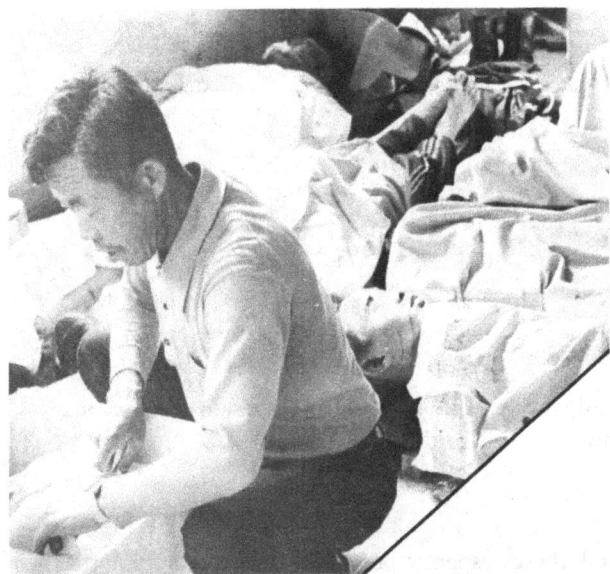

Bodies being prepared in the Chonnam University Hospital morgue.

Bodies outside the Chonnam University Hospital morgue.

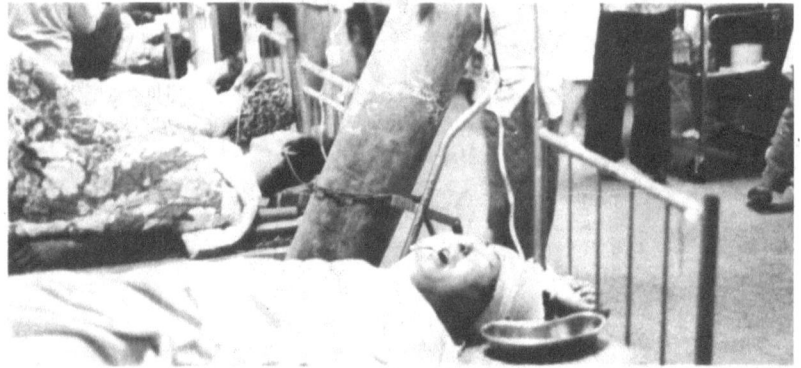

The wounded from the first four days of the uprising, overflowing into makeshift wards at Chonnam University Hospital.

It was hard to watch these desperate people who were searching for their loved ones, and who, thinking that they recognized a pant leg, pulled back the sheet only to find that it wasn't their child.

What was most heart-rending, however, was hearing the tortured cries of people the moment they discovered their child among the dead. The mothers would begin to wail in grief if they were present, but these cries usually came from fathers searching for their sons. The men would begin to weep and speak to their dead children as if they were carrying on a conversation with them, telling them they should not have died, that they had no right to die before their parents. They would apologize for being such a bad parent and promise that if only the child would come back, they would do better. Witnessing this scene ripped my soul to its core. Their cries were sounds that no one should ever have to make, and no one should ever have to hear.

After they had gotten photos of the morgue, the reporters took their leave. Tim, Judi, and I left the hospital and walked by the burnt-out shell of the MBC building. We were told that it had been burnt down by protesters two nights earlier because MBC's broadcasts had lied about what was happening in Kwangju. Not far away was the tax office, which had also been burned down around the same time. People in Jeollanam-do had long been angry that their taxes were used by the government to help other provinces rather than their own, but now their taxes were being used to kill them.

Near the MBC building, in the middle of the street, was a small exhibit of photos affixed to a wooden board. The photos, which were in color and black and white, showed the bodies of citizens killed by the paratroopers. Standing around the exhibit were students who explained the photos and used a bullhorn to draw people's attention. No words could describe just how gruesome and unbelievable the photographs were. It was hard to tell, at first, that some of the pictures were of people. What we saw were no longer recognizable as faces; the features weren't in the right places. There was also a picture of a young woman with her abdomen slashed open. One of the young men told us that she was pregnant and after the paratroopers killed her, they had cut open her belly and removed the fetus. We did not see a picture of the fetus or anything else to support this, however. There was also a picture of a young woman with her breasts slashed off. To this day, I still can't get those images out of my head, nor understand what would make someone do that to another human being.

We continued to wander around the city so we could see what was happening. We visited a market to see if there was a lack of food for sale, but there wasn't. In fact, most of the stalls were open. Then we walked back to Tim's for a quick lunch. Sun-jae's mother also confirmed that she wasn't aware of any food shortages.

In the early afternoon Tim suggested we call Seoul to alert the Peace Corps and the U.S. Embassy as to what was happening in Kwangju and to convey the fact that the military had killed so many innocent people. We all agreed it was a good idea and thought the U.S. Embassy might be concerned and want firsthand information. We walked to a public phone booth just down the street from the MBC building.

I didn't know the number for the Peace Corps office or the Embassy, so Tim made the call. I didn't hear the full conversation, but before long Tim paused and told us that he was being told that we should leave the city immediately because our safety was threatened by the "rioters." It had never occurred to us to leave the city and we saw no reason to do so. After a quick discussion among ourselves, Tim told them they were completely wrong about what was happening and that we were safer in the city with the citizens of Kwangju than dealing with the soldiers. He said we saw no reason to leave the city and that we wanted to stay to make sure our friends were okay.

They thought we should be farther away from downtown and told us to go to the home of the USIS[10] director. We were told there should be a housekeeper present who would let us in, and from there we could use a secure phone to call Seoul. Tim knew where the house was, so we walked over but found no one home and the gate locked. Since we had been told to go there and use the secure phone, we tried to see if we could get in somehow but had no luck. We went back to the pay phone to call Seoul again.

On our way, we discussed whether our actions so far had violated our Peace Corps oath, which stated that we should not engage in political activity. We agreed they hadn't, because our activities had nothing to do with politics but rather concern for our friends and the citizens of Kwangju. For me, walking away would be morally wrong, and I said that we should stay to bear witness and provide statements about what was happening in Kwangju. At that time, I naïvely believed that the U.S.

---

10   United States Information Service

Thousands of citizens gathered for the afternoon rallies in front of the Provincial Capital.

government would act to stop what was happening if it knew the truth. We came to a consensus and decided to act as one in our discussions with the Peace Corps and U.S. Embassy. Once we were on the phone with Seoul again, they tried to convince us to leave immediately by walking out. We each took the phone and individually stated that we were not leaving.

Later in the afternoon we returned to the Provincial Capital. We had learned that there was going to be a rally there and wanted to see it. The traffic circle in front of the Provincial Capital building was packed with thousands of people. Speakers were set up and various people climbed up onto the fountain in the center of the traffic circle to speak. As each person took the microphone, they stated their name and then expressed their anger and frustration at what had happened. Some were old, some young, some were students, and others were businessmen and community elders, but there was a feeling of unity and harmony among the people. There was a strong will not to lose what they had fought and sacrificed for and what others had died for. The rally included a memorial for some of the citizens who had died, and 15 coffins were brought into the square.

During the rally, we saw a man being escorted toward the fountain. As he was led through the crowd, people spat at him and tried to hit him, but he was well-protected by the young men leading him. He'd been captured by citizens because he was suspected of being a north Korean spy. I asked a couple of the people around me about him and they said he had been caught spying and was suspected of being from north Korea, so he was going to be turned over to the military at the Settlement Committee's next meeting with them.

As the rally continued, the Settlement Committee leaders took the podium and introduced themselves by name and explained who they were. They then explained the demands they had put forth in their negotiations with the military that afternoon, and what the military was demanding in return. One of the military's main demands was the collection and turning over of the weapons that had been seized by the citizens. This demand caused a great deal of debate. The 15 members of the citizens' committee were lawyers, clergymen, professors, and businessmen and tended to agree that the guns should be collected and returned to the military. Some students and workers disagreed and argued that their possession of firearms and continued resistance was the only reason the military had not already tried to retake the city. The disagreement among these groups on the podium was obvious as they argued over how to respond to the military's demands.

Eventually a scuffle broke out. We were at the outer edge of the crowd, and because the din of the crowd had increased by this point, it was difficult to hear, even with the PA system. From what I found out later, the scuffle was because as a committee they were not fully in agreement on how they should negotiate with the military, but some members tried to get their way by announcing their plan to the crowd as if the committee had already agreed on it. Another point of contention for the younger people was that the older members of the committee seemed willing to do whatever the military wanted. People in the crowd were clearly still angry about the paratroopers' brutality, as they began to shout when the elders called for yielding to the military's demands. A student eventually suggested that a Student Settlement Committee be formed, and student leaders left to undertake this.

Near the end of the rally, a young man behind us greeted us in Korean and we began speaking with him. We learned that he was 17, had not graduated from middle school, worked various jobs, including as a rag picker, and lived on the streets. Perhaps because we were American, he showed us a CS gas grenade canister that had been used against protesters. It had "Made in the U.S.A." stenciled on the side. He said that a number of people had been hit in the head by the canisters and that he had seen a young man killed this way.

We stayed in the square for a while after the rally ended to find out more about the members of the committee and the negotiations. After returning to Tim's for dinner, we decided to go check in on a close friend of Tim's who was in hiding. He was a poet and dissident who had been on the arrest list for the night of May 17 but was lucky enough to have eluded capture. To get there we took a very circuitous route and constantly checked to make sure we weren't being followed. We found him safe, but fearful, and making plans to leave the city. He needed toiletries, so I went to a nearby store to get him a toothbrush, toothpaste, and some snacks. Having confirmed that he was all right, we left after 15 minutes.

Soon after we returned to Tim's we were surprised when Paul Courtright, a PCV based in Naju County, walked in. That a PCV would come visit Tim was not surprising, since Kwangju was Tim's city, and he was generous and open enough to share his address with the other PCVs. We just didn't expect to see anyone else coming into Kwangju. Paul told us he had ridden his bicycle past military blockades to get into the city. After sharing stories of what we had experienced the past few days, we all went to bed.

That night there was a strange and eerie silence in Kwangju broken only by occasional gunshots coming from the outskirts of the city.

8. Doing What We Can

Friday, May 23

We awoke the next morning and had breakfast, though I didn't eat much. I was more interested in having coffee, which in those days was of the instant variety and which Sun-jae's mother would make for us and serve in small cups. I was still trying to process the events of the past few days. I wanted to get back out on the streets to see what was happening and try to help reporters who needed interpreters. Tim, Judi, Paul, and I decided to walk to the Provincial Capital together.

On the way, we saw people out cleaning the streets again. When we arrived at the Provincial Capital, we saw that the call for weapons to be turned in at the previous day's rally was having an effect. Though this demand by the military had led to a great deal of arguing between those who agreed or disagreed with it, many people had clearly decided to abide by it. Citizens were bringing firearms to the gate of the Provincial Capital to turn them in, and the pile of weapons inside and to the left of the gate grew larger as jeep-loads of them were brought in by people who had driven around the city to collect them from more distant neighborhoods.

This was also the first time I saw women handing out rice balls to citizens who were in the Provincial Capital buildings or patrolling the streets. The rice balls were carried in baskets, and I also saw them transported in pull-carts and jeeps. It was quite common to see people sharing in this way. The food was prepared communally for the citizens who were defending and running the city, but they also approached us to share them when we were walking in the streets. I suppose my habit of always being polite, bowing, and saying hello if people made eye-contact helped, but I also think some of these older women thought I looked too thin and were worried about my health.

Not long after arriving at the Provincial Capital building, Paul decided to leave Kwangju. He had told us the previous evening that he had plans to go to Taiwan the following week and needed to get to Seoul within the next few days. We wished him luck before he headed off to Tim's to get his bike.

It was mid-morning but already there were crowds of people milling about and sitting on the pavement in front of the Provincial Capital building. That atmosphere was quite calm. Many of them were waiting to hear updates on what was happening. We asked around and learned that the earlier-formed citizen settlement committee and the new student committee had held a discussion the previous night that was rumored to have involved a great deal of debate and argument. It was clear that many of the young people involved did not trust the military.

Tim, Judi, and I decided to sit down in front of the gate to the Provincial Capital as we waited for more updates. Before long, a news crew came by and started filming the scene, but because they were Japanese, they received a different reaction than Western news crews. People started shouting that everyone should hide their faces because the government was using this kind of footage to identify people. Despite the suspicion directed at the Japanese reporters, they were given friendlier treatment than the Korean reporters, who were sometimes criticized or yelled at due to the citizens' anger at the dishonest and biased news broadcasts coming from Seoul.

After waiting for some time without any updates, we decided to visit Chonnam University Hospital again to see what was happening there, and to find out if the emergency room was dealing with any serious cases from the previous evening. The situation was like that of the previous day: the hallways were full of patients and the doctors told us no beds were free. While we were in the emergency room, Tim ran into some friends who were being treated for minor gunshot wounds. It turned out they were deaf, and Tim surprised me when he began using sign language to speak with them. I told Tim I was impressed, but he replied modestly that he only knew a little sign language.

After grabbing some lunch at Tim's, we walked back to the Provincial Capital to attend the afternoon rally. By now people had learned that the rally was the place to go to learn about the progress of the negotiations, and since the situation in the city was much calmer, more people were making their way downtown to find out what was happening. It was hard to judge how many people were there from our vantage point at the edge of the crowd, but there were more people than on Thursday. Much like the previous day, the rally began with the gathered citizens singing the national anthem. The songs I had heard chanted by the young men in the buses and trucks on May 21 calling for Chun Doo-hwan to step down and demanding Kim Dae-jung be freed were no longer sung after Kwangju's citizens took control of the city.

Members of the citizens' committee told the crowd how the negotiations with the military were progressing, explained what the military's demands were, and made clear that these demands kept changing. Key among these was the collection of weapons, a topic that continued to inspire debate between those who thought that the committee should do what the military wanted, and those who opposed this. These discussions occurred not only among the committee members, but also among the people in the audience. From our vantage point in the crowd, it seemed that people were very interested in the negotiations and were hoping for a peaceful resolution.

At the rally that day we met Terry Anderson, who wrote for the Associated Press, and Robin Moyer, a photographer for *Time* magazine. After briefly discussing what we had seen over the past few days, they invited us to meet them at the inn where they were staying so we could share what we had seen and experienced in more detail. We agreed to meet them that evening. When the rally ended, we walked back to Tim's place for dinner.

While we were eating, we were surprised to see Paul return. He told us he had been turned back at a military roadblock on the outskirts of the city. Even though he had told the soldiers that he was a Peace Corps Volunteer trying to return home, they had refused to let him leave the city. Since we knew reporters were getting in, we were surprised by this, especially since he was headed southwest toward Naju and not north toward Seoul. What was more startling was the fact that they had refused to allow an American PCV who spoke Korean to pass, since our Peace Corps status and ability to speak Korean usually allowed us to do things that Koreans could not. Much like everything else that was happening, this was highly abnormal.

After dinner, we left to go meet the journalists. The inn they were staying at was next to the Provincial Capital building, so we walked over and went up to their room to talk. From their window we could look out onto the side and back of the Provincial Capital buildings. As it was a Korean-style inn, we sat on the floor. Tim led the conversation since he lived in Kwangju and had witnessed the most, while the rest of us added in details and contributed our own stories when necessary.

That night and in the following days, I was somewhat taken aback by how detached the journalists seemed when they responded to the stories we shared or when they talked about what was happening. With so many bodies in the morgues and brutal photos being displayed, I imagined this was partly a coping mechanism, but it just seemed to me like they were more interested in telling a possibly prize-winning story than in trying to fully understand the depth of the issues. Many of the journalists were writing for American audiences. As a result, though they knew that the military had acted with great brutality, their U.S.-centric viewpoint led them to look for an American connection to the story because I think they knew the deaths of so many non-Americans wouldn't really resonate with their readers.

After we had spoken with the journalists for some time, a young college student, who was a spokesperson for the Settlement Committee, came to their door and asked if we would be willing to interpret for him as he spoke to the journalists. We agreed. Tim did most of the interpreting, and I helped clarify things as needed as we went back and forth in Korean and English.

He said he wanted the journalists to report the facts of what was happening, but he also wanted them to make sure the U.S. Embassy and the U.S. government learned the truth about the situation in Kwangju. He felt that the journalists were the only means to get the U.S. government to intervene and ensure that there would be no more bloodshed. In response, the journalists stated that they could only explain what was happening through their newspaper reports. They said they could not go directly to the U.S. government to express the committee's desire for it to intervene because that would be outside the scope of their role as independent observers. The young man ended up leaving frustrated. I think in some ways he saw the journalists as the last hope for a peaceful outcome.

After the spokesperson left, we continued speaking with the journalists, and they made it clear that they didn't agree with the citizens asking them to contact the U.S. Embassy directly. They also expressed their belief that the military would return eventually, in part because the citizens didn't seem to know what they were doing, weren't unified, and couldn't agree on what an acceptable outcome would be.

We wrapped up our conversation and started to leave, but then realized it was after 9 p.m. and curfew had begun. The journalists offered to pay for extra rooms at the inn so we could spend the night there, which we accepted gratefully. Tim, Paul, and I slept in one room, and Judi slept in the other. Though we were staying at an inn, for me it was just another floor to sleep on, since I have never slept well when I am away from home. Once the lights were out, I eventually drifted off to sleep.

9. A Day in Their Shoes
Saturday, May 24

W hen we woke up the next morning, Tim decided to return home to check in with his host family. I went with him and ate a quick breakfast with Sun-jae and his mother, who had been concerned by our absence. We returned to the Provincial Capital by 10 a.m. Just like the previous day, there were many people gathered in the square near the fountain. Some had been there for an hour or more wanting to hear updates, to find out how they could help, or to learn if additional bodies had been found or identified.

Tim and I found Judi and Paul talking with reporters, including Terry Anderson, Robin Moyer, and Jürgen Hinzpeter, a German reporter and cameraman. He and his assistant joined us as we walked together to the gate of the Provincial Capital. Several armed students and young men were guarding the gate, and one of them asked if we had passes. Since we didn't, he asked why we were there, and let us in when he realized our group consisted of reporters and interpreters. As we walked in, I noticed that the size of the pile of collected weapons hadn't changed much since the previous day.

Tim, Judi, Paul, and I split up so we could interpret for as many reporters as possible. One young man explained that he joined the uprising since he felt he had no other choice because of the indiscriminate use of violence by the paratroopers against the people of his city. He said they had needed to take up arms to defend themselves and because protesting non-violently would have just gotten them killed.

Before long we all gathered in a meeting room on the second floor to talk with people from the settlement committee. It was difficult to ascertain how the committee wanted to proceed, however, because it had divided into factions. Though everyone wanted a peaceful outcome, they could not agree on how to achieve this. The older community leaders who had initially formed the committee wanted a quick end to the turmoil and a return to normalcy. Many thought that in their rush to comply with the military's demands, they were not listening to the diverse views of the citizens that the committee was supposed to be representing. The younger, recently added committee members were not willing to compromise if it was at the expense of the lives that had been sacrificed. They wanted amnesty for the citizens who had been involved and wanted the military and government to admit fault and to admit to the extreme violence of their tactics. It became clear that neither side was willing to back down from their positions.

We left the Provincial Capital together with the reporters. We spoke with Jürgen Hinzpeter some more, and when he realized how much we had seen of the uprising, he asked if he could interview one of us. The four of us discussed it and agreed, deciding that Tim would do the interview and speak for us all because he had witnessed events from the very beginning. During the discussion we told Hinzpeter that as PCVs we could not be "politically involved" and that we were worried that being interviewed in this way might be defined as political involvement by the Peace Corps. It was decided that Tim would be identified as someone who worked for an NGO. I later learned that when the interview was broadcast in Germany, his identity as a PCV was obscured by stating that he worked for Amnesty International.

Since Hinzpeter was interested in finding a tall rooftop to film from, Tim suggested doing the interview on the rooftop of Chonnam University Hospital. The other reporters wanted to interview doctors and patients at the hospital, so they joined us. Paul, Judi, and I accompanied Tim, Hinzpeter, and his assistant to the roof and watched as they set up the interview. Someone captured that moment on film, though I'm not sure who.

On the roof of Chonnam University Hospital just prior to Tim being interviewed by Jürgen Hinzpeter. From left to right: Jürgen Hinzpeter, Henning Rumohr, Judi Chamberlin, Tim Warnberg, Paul Courtright, and David Dolinger.

Hinzpeter then began filming Tim as he described the things he had witnessed. Judi decided to stay for the interview, while Paul and I went downstairs and split up to help interpret for the other reporters. Overcrowding was still a problem and we walked past patients lying in beds in the hallways. The doctors wanted to show reporters the wounded and dead, and to answer questions, but were not willing to provide their names. I made sure that the reporters understood that the doctors feared retribution after the military regained control of the city. We were able to go wherever we wanted and talk with the wounded, their families, and doctors and nurses. Some of the patients we talked to were young people who had been wounded while manning the barricades. We counted about 30 bodies in and outside the overwhelmed morgue. Once again, I heard the wails of people discovering their loved ones among the victims, a scene I'd witnessed too many times. It was always difficult to hear the heart-rending cries of a parent who had lost their child.

After Tim wrapped up his interview and Paul and I finished translating for the journalists, we all gathered outside the hospital and walked back toward the Provincial Capital. We decided to see if we could enter the Sangmugwan, a gymnasium across from the Provincial Capital that was being used as a temporary resting place for bodies that had been identified. Though they had been claimed by families, the families had allowed their loved ones to rest with the other fallen until a memorial service could be arranged. Joined by one or two journalists, we had to ask to be let into the building because it was not open to the general public at the time. The air inside was filled with incense which was being burned in large quantities to try to mask the smell of death, with only partial success. There the deceased were all in closed coffins that were lined up in rows on the blue floor of the gymnasium. Most of the coffins had a name written on the lid and many had photos of the dead and flowers resting on top. Some had family members sitting around them who were keeping vigil. We counted over a hundred coffins there.

Upon leaving the gymnasium, the journalists thanked us for our help and parted from us. After we wandered around for a bit, I decided to go for a walk by myself so I could gather my thoughts. I returned to the Provincial Capital in time for that afternoon's rally at 3 p.m.

Being on the ground made it hard to determine the size of the crowd; it was later estimated that there were about 50,000 people at this particular rally. By this point the divide on the committee between the elder citizens who hoped things would go back to normal by compromising with the military and the younger people and students who wanted more concessions from the military was obvious. In fact, the Settlement Committee tried to cut off power to the PA system, so there was a delay in starting the rally as students found another set of speakers.

From the people I talked to, and from the mood of the crowd, it was clear that most of the citizens present were still upset over the military's brutality and the resulting deaths. They wanted a peaceful resolution but also wanted the military and the government to admit their fault, provide compensation to those who had lost loved ones, and provide amnesty for those involved, including letting everyone who was in custody go free. As a result, there was a lot of booing and yelling from the crowd that drowned out the members of the Settlement Committee when they tried to speak. A sudden downpour interrupted the rally briefly, but people returned to watch an effigy of Chun Doo-hwan be set on fire. NBC, and perhaps other journalists, filmed the rally.

After the rally finished, I began talking with a young man outside the Provincial Capital. We discussed what was happening at the rally as well as the general situation in Kwangju. I introduced myself using both my Korean and American names; for the rest of that evening he used my Korean name whenever he addressed me. He introduced himself as Jang Gye-beom, and as it turned out, he was a member of the group of students in the Provincial Capital who were trying to run the city. I think because I spoke Korean and was sympathetic to their cause, he asked me if I would like to see what was happening in the Provincial Capital. I replied that I would. We then walked through the gate and he provided me with a pass that would allow me into the Provincial Capital buildings whenever I wanted. The pass was a two-by-three-inch[11] piece of brownish recycled paper stamped three times with the Chinese character for "secret."

Jang then led me inside the main building and into a room just to the left of the entrance. We sat at a desk and he talked about how the students were trying to run the city in the absence of the government. He also explained how they were trying to negotiate a way out of the situation, but the military was not negotiating in good faith. He also believed that the military was trying to create divisions between the older citizen leaders and student members of the settlement committee. From there, the conversation turned to my being Quaker. I explained that, due to my beliefs, I could not support the use of violence by the military or the citizens. While I understood the response of the citizens, I would have resisted peacefully through civil disobedience. When he asked for clarification, I told him that I would not have done anything to harm the paratroopers, and I would have been willing to be beaten. For someone who had undergone mandatory military service in a country that had lived through a war not long ago, it was difficult for him to comprehend this stance.

Jang then offered to show me around the Provincial Capital. We walked outside and he showed me where they were storing the weapons that had been collected. We then walked over to the annex building to the left of the main building where he pointed to a door and told me it led to

---

11 Two-by-three inches is about five-by-eight centimeters.

a basement where over 600 bodies were being stored. I was not shown the bodies, but in conversations with other students there I was told the same thing, though the exact number of bodies differed depending on whom I was talking to. Jang then showed me the first and second floors of the main building and explained how the defenses were set up. He also pointed out the different offices that the students and activists had taken over so they could run the city. They had been divided into teams to organize defense, transportation, and public relations.

After talking for some time, Jang asked me if I would be willing to help by bearing witness to what was happening in the Provincial Capital. I said yes. He first asked if I could provide some advice regarding the authenticity of foreign reporters' press credentials and had me examine the passport of a Korean-Japanese reporter to determine if it was real. I read through the passport, looked for errors in any of the English, checked to make sure that there was an embossed stamp, and told him I thought it was real. He told me that he was curious as to whether the journalist could be a north Korean sympathizer. The fact that most of the Japanese journalists in the city were fluent in Korean made clear they were Korean-Japanese. Having been told that a significant number of Koreans in Japan were loyal to north Korea, he was worried that these reporters might be north Korean agents or sympathizers. The students didn't want to be associated with these kinds of people because they were afraid their presence in the city could be used to smear Kwangju's citizens as communists. There was also fear that these journalists' broadcasts might be distorted or feature a bias toward north Korea. I told him that kind of affiliation would not be reflected in the passport, but it was a possibility.

After about an hour had passed, Jang invited me to attend a meeting by the student committee that was to begin soon. We discussed some of the issues involved with the military's stance, and how they kept changing their demands and making them more restrictive every day. I told him I didn't think that the military ever planned to negotiate in good faith because they had been humiliated by their retreat from the city. I thought they were biding their time and hoping to create dissention in the Provincial Capital, in order to make re-taking the city easier for them. I was about to get a firsthand look at just how much division already existed.

Jang led me upstairs to a small office which we passed through to gain entry to a much larger meeting room. There were at least ten people already sitting around tables that had been pushed together. I sat down with my back to the front wall of the building, which faced the main street, and Jang sat to my right. We were waiting for the meeting to begin when a group of people walked in and sat down. One of them looked directly at me and asked, "Who is the foreigner?" Jang quickly replied that he had asked me to bear witness to what was happening in the Provincial Capital building and to observe the citizens' committee. I told him my Korean name and explained that I was a Peace Corps Volunteer who lived in Yeongam. He introduced himself as Yun Sang-won. It quickly became clear that he was regarded as the leader of the group, because when another person suggested that I should not be allowed to remain for the meeting, Yun said it was fine and put an end to the discussion.

With that they got down to business and began discussing the negotiations with the military. Though the meeting only involved the students and activists, not the older community leaders who were more willing to compromise with the government, the division between the soft and hard-line factions among those present was clear for all to see. The two sides soon began shouting at one another over the issue of handing over weapons to the military. The hard-liners did not trust the military and argued that the only reason they had not yet been attacked was because they still had weapons. The soft-liners didn't really do much to make their point other than to say that the military was going to attack if the weapons weren't handed in and then a lot of people would die. No compromise was reached on this issue. Yun Sang-won and the other hard-liners were certain there was going to be no peaceful ending and had resolved to hold out as long as possible to protect the city. For them, an important question was how to minimize the inevitable bloodshed. They also wondered if they could hold out long enough for the rest of Korea to recognize what was happening, and whether this knowledge could provoke the rest of the country to join in their resistance against the new dictatorship.

The hard-liners made clear their belief that the military only saw the negotiations as a delaying tactic and that they would attack before long; the question was how soon. They believed that if the military was going to attack, it would be early in the morning before daybreak. Talk quickly turned to the barricade situation and whether any troop movements had been observed. Jang took part in a discussion about perimeter defenses, and then the conversation turned to the monitoring of military radio frequencies.

The Provincial Capital was equipped with a military radio that they had been listening to in order to determine if the soldiers were going to attack the city. While discussing plans to man the radio that night, the idea that the soldiers might use English to coordinate the attack was brought up, as was the possibility that the U.S. military could be involved. In response, Jang suggested that having someone who spoke English monitor the radio might be a good idea. Yun agreed and asked if I would be willing to help man the radio that night. Without any hesitation, I said yes. I felt that it was a minor thing to do and that it could potentially save lives. As the meeting broke up and we were all leaving the room, Yun stopped me and said, "Now you are a citizen of Kwangju." Looking back, one of my fondest memories of May 1980 was being told that I was viewed as a citizen of Kwangju because of what I was willing to do.

At around 9 p.m., when I was to begin monitoring the radio, Jang told me he was heading off to attend another student committee meeting. I hadn't eaten dinner because I wasn't hungry and was just drinking water. This may have been partly influenced by hearing people in the Provincial Capital building talk about how they hadn't slept and couldn't remember if they'd eaten or not.

The radio was set up in what I remember to be the Provincial Capital's library, which was at the west end of the main building. This was the wing of the building that the reporters could see from their inn. The radio was at the back of the library, away from the front wall. The lights were off in the room, as they were throughout most of the building to make it difficult for the military to target the people inside. Joining me in the radio room were two other people. One was a Chonnam University student, and the other was a man in his mid- to- late 40s who had retired to Kwangju after 20 years of service in the military. He had been a master sergeant and was married and had children. He made a great impression on me. He was shorter than me, but had a very strong presence, both in the way he carried himself and in the way he spoke. I could see why the students respected him, but he also had a kind and gentle side that manifested in the way he spoke with me.

We talked for much of the night, but I spent most of the time listening to him as he explained why he had to do what he was doing and why the citizens of Kwangju were compelled to fight back. The government had no right to act this way, he said. Even though he was a former soldier, he felt he had no choice but to get involved after he had seen what the paratroopers were doing to his fellow citizens. Up to this point, however, he had taken part not by fighting, but by using his knowledge to help and guide those who were. He talked about his life, his family, his children, and said that he was doing his part because he wanted to make Korea a better place. He told me he was not afraid to die if sacrificing his life would bring about a better future for his children and the country. This was a common theme among those I spoke to in the Provincial Capital building, including the young people who were willing to resist the military.

Throughout the night we scanned the military radio frequencies trying to determine if the soldiers were going to attack. Though we occasionally heard the military communicating over the radio, they did not invade that night. If they had, my plan was not to fight, but also not to run. I intended to go to the square in front of the Provincial Capital to sit down and wait. I figured I would probably be arrested and sent to prison. I didn't think they would shoot an unarmed, round-eyed American, which was probably a very foolish thing to believe. I wasn't really concerned because I thought I was doing the right thing and believed that was what mattered the most.

At around 11 p.m. we sucked down raw eggs to keep our strength up. At one point I slouched down in a chair and took a 10- or 15-minute nap. I woke up in the dark to the sight of the student and former soldier illuminated by the radio dial and the glow of the older man's cigarette. The rest of the night passed uneventfully.

10. Can it Last?

Sunday, May 25

I saw the sky begin to lighten through the windows of the library. Once the sun had fully risen and there was enough light to keep tabs on the military visually, the former soldier called an end to the manning of the radio. He told us to get something to eat. I replied that I had to get home to let my friends know that I was all right. My companions said that after eating they were going to try to get some sleep elsewhere in the Provincial Capital building. I thanked them and told them I hoped to see them again.

We parted and I walked out of the building and toward the gate. The guards were surprised to see a foreigner coming out that early in the morning, especially when I greeted them in Korean. I walked across the square and headed to Tim's. When I arrived, I told the others how I had spent the night. Tim had been quite concerned because he hadn't known where I was, but he also wanted to hear more about what was happening inside the Provincial Capital, so over breakfast I shared what I had seen and heard.

As we sat on the floor of the main room, we watched some news reports about what was happening in Kwangju, but they just made us angry because of the false picture they painted. In contrast to the description of a city beset by chaos, there was never any looting, and there were no shortages at that point. People were sharing food, and while the open-air markets had fewer and fewer goods, you could still find rice and people were not over-charging for it.

Paul decided that after the memorial service he was going to try once again to leave Kwangju and make his way to Seoul. We had shared with him our accounts of what we had witnessed, and he planned to convey them to the Peace Corps director, with the hope that this information would be passed on to the U.S. ambassador.

After breakfast we all walked over to the Provincial Capital. There weren't as many people gathered out front as there had been in days past. We met up with a number of journalists, but our plans to attend a memorial service for the fallen at the Sangmugwan were changed by the postponement of the service until the next day. I was told that the reason for the delay was the committee's decision to wait until additional bodies were identified and permission was received from the families to include them in the memorial service.

With the memorial postponed, some of the journalists decided they wanted to visit churches so they could get pictures of some of the morning services. We decided to split up so we could help as many of the reporters as possible. I accompanied one of the journalists to several churches.

During the morning services there was a strong focus on those who had given their lives, and there were also prayers for the citizens' militia who were protecting the city. A priest who was interviewed at one church focused on the people who had fallen and worried about what the final outcome would be. Though the services were not well-attended, there was a calmness I felt being in the churches, as if my worries had been left behind at the door. Due to the focus of the service and our conversations with people in the congregation, however, it wasn't possible to leave Kwangju's predicament behind completely. It was clear the people attending the service were focused on praying for a peaceful resolution.

After the services we walked back toward the Provincial Capital, arriving there around 11:30 a.m. The journalist I was with decided he wanted to go out to the perimeter where the citizens' militia was guarding the city. As he only wanted to take photos, he told me he didn't need any help with interpretation. I found him a ride in a jeep that was headed that way.

After he left, I ran into Tim in the square. He had also just parted ways with the journalist he was accompanying. Since Tim and I were both interested in seeing what was happening in the Provincial Capital, we walked over to the front gate. I showed the guard my pass and told him Tim was with me, and he let us in. As we approached the building it became clear something had happened because the place was in an uproar. People were screaming at each other and questioning each other, while others were running in and out of the building.

I asked one of the students what was happening and learned that someone had been stabbed and that poison may have been involved. It was suspected that the military might have been behind it, so while some people were searching the building, others were being ordered out to the perimeter in the belief that the stabbing could be a prelude to an attack. I decided to track down Jang to get more information and asked a young man I had met the previous day where he was. He told me that it was Jang who had been stabbed in the back, possibly by a government agent with a pen, and that they also thought there was poison in the pen. We learned that he had been taken to Chonnam University Hospital.

Tim and I took off and ran over to the hospital. When we got to the ER, we told the doctor that we knew the patient and were worried about him, so the ER doctor told us what he knew. There was no poison; Jang had simply been stabbed with a pen and was suffering from exhaustion, so he had been sent home. The doctor mentioned that as he was being released, Jang had told the ER staff that he had dynamite at home and would not be taken alive by the military. The doctor wrote down Jang's name and address for us. As I thought it would be better for him to rest at home, we didn't go to check on him.

After the stabbing, the possibility that a government agent might have been involved created a lot of paranoia and confusion in the Provincial Capital compound, and rumors that the military was tightening its encirclement of the city only added to this. Some people I talked to felt that the government was trying to create panic so it could more easily justify the soldiers re-entering the city. In fact, the suspicion that the government was trying to divide people was a topic Jang and I had discussed the previous evening.

Sunday afternoon saw another rally held in front of the Provincial Capital building and a march of solidarity through the streets. It rained, and many people told me that the rain was the tears of God falling for the citizens of Kwangju. The crowd appeared smaller than those of the previous days. Unlike on previous days, the crowd on Sunday only fit into the square and was not spread up Geumnam-ro and overflowing into the side streets. I think one reason for this was that the citizens had realized that little progress was being made toward a peaceful resolution, and out of concern for this they were becoming more cautious.

At the rally, groups of people confronted me and Tim and angrily demanded to know if General Wickham[12] had authorized the use of troops to suppress the people of Kwangju, and asked us if the U.S. government was supporting the Chun regime. They also wanted to know if the aircraft carrier the United States had dispatched to Korea was meant to support the people of Kwangju or Chun Doo-hwan. They were upset, and being Korean-speaking Americans we had to take the brunt of their anger. It was clear, however, that they were not angry at us personally but were just directing their confusion and frustration at us. We were finally able to convince them that we didn't know anything about it and had no leverage over the U.S. government, but that we had communicated with the U.S. Embassy to tell them the truth of what was happening in Kwangju and that we were not going to leave the city. When they finally left us, we could see that they believed us, but were frustrated with the U.S. government. They wondered how a government that had built its foreign policy around human rights could abandon people who had been brutalized and who only wanted a peaceful outcome.

Some of this frustration was reflected in the mood of the rally. Taking the microphone, members of the committee who sounded more hardline argued that the military was not negotiating in good faith and kept altering its terms and requirements, and stated that the committee was not going to accept this. They made it clear that they were not going to bend to the military's demands and that they were willing to give their lives.

When the rally ended, Tim and Judi decided to visit the American missionaries who lived in a compound south of the city center. They apparently knew the missionaries quite well, and Judi had already stopped in to see them on several occasions during the previous few days. I decided

---

12 General Wickham: General John A. Wickham served as Commander of United States Forces, Korea (USFK), as well as Commander in Chief of United Nations Command (UNC) and United States-Republic of Korea Combined Forces Command (CFC) from July 1979 to June 1982. As CFC commander, Wickham had to acknowledge or approve removal of ROK troops from CFC operational control (OPCON); the paratroopers used in Kwangju were never under CFC control, however. On May 24, KBS (under the control of ROK military censors) broadcast into Kwangu reports that the US had encouraged the use of troops in the city, a "distortion" that Wickham protested, and this was the likely source of the citizens' anger.

to go into the Provincial Capital to say hello to the people I had manned the radio with and to find out what was happening. I had no luck finding the student or the former soldier from the previous night, but I did learn more about the events of the past day. Conversations I had in the Provincial Capital and statements made at the rally made it clear that the hardline group led by Yun Sang-won was now in charge. The meeting held after I had left to monitor the radio Saturday night had resulted in many of the more moderate students resigning from the committee and being replaced with activists and workers unwilling to give in to the military's demands.

After spending some time talking to people in the Provincial Capital, I decided it had been a long day and headed back to Tim's for dinner. There I found Tim and Judi in a state of nervous agitation and worry. While they were visiting the missionaries, they received a report that the military was tightening its encirclement of the city and had advanced right up to the edge of the missionary compound. Upon hearing this, Tim and Judi had quickly left and returned home. Throughout Sunday we had heard more and more talk of the military re-entering the city. By Sunday night we were worried that the military would attack early Monday morning.

We went to bed at 10 p.m. and, tired by the events of the past two days, I quickly dropped off to sleep. At around 10:30 p.m. we were awakened by the ringing of the phone in the main room. It was for Tim, and he was told it was from someone at Chosun University Hospital who was calling to tell him that one of his friends had been brought into the emergency room and was in critical condition. Though curfew had begun at 9 p.m., Tim said that this person was a very close friend and that he had to go to the hospital. Without hesitating, I offered to go with him. We put on our shoes and jogged through the deserted streets from Tim's house to Chosun University Hospital, which included an uphill climb as we neared our destination. The streetlights were on, but citizens had covered their windows, something we did every night to minimize the light. We burst into the ER, expecting to see chaos, but it was quiet. There were no people waiting for treatment, only a few nurses and doctors. They told us that there had been no emergencies that night. Perhaps we were mistaken, and our friend was at Chonnam University Hospital.

Off we went again, this time running down the hill as we made our way to Chonnam University Hospital. As we entered the ER there, however, we were once again greeted by calm. There had been no real emergencies that night and certainly no gunshot wounds. We were perplexed and tried to talk through what had just happened. Who had called, and how did they know the name of Tim's friend? Was the house being watched? Did someone want to grab Tim, or did they just want him out of the house? Why call so late, and weren't the phone lines down? To this day I am still without any closure on this matter. As we walked back to Tim's in the middle of the wide, empty street, we asked each other many questions but could find no answers.

About halfway back to Tim's, a jeep came speeding up to us. In it were two college students carrying M-1s, and we immediately wondered if they knew what was going on and were seeking us out. But that wasn't the case at all. When they saw us, they said hello and asked if we wanted a ride. Despite it being after curfew, we declined because we wanted to keep talking about what had happened. With that, they told us to be safe and took off down the road toward the barricades on the outskirts of the city.

We spent the rest of the walk home talking over what had just happened. We got back to Tim's without incident, and it was nice to be able to relax once we were indoors again. We told the others that everything was okay, that it was just a false alarm. We then went back to bed and, being exhausted, I quickly fell asleep.

11. Funerals and Farewells
Monday, May 26

We awoke Monday morning to an unchanged situation; the military had not re-entered the city. Sun-jae's mother told us that some food items were becoming scarce at the market, but one reason for this was that some of the merchants had been giving food away to ensure that the citizens' militia was fed. After breakfast, Tim and Judi decided to go check in on the missionaries to see if there was any news. We agreed to meet later downtown.

I walked over to the Provincial Capital to try to find out what was happening. I stopped at the foreign reporters' inn first to see if they had any news. I then went over to the Provincial Capital building, where I ended up spending most of my day. I found out from my conversations there that earlier in the morning the soldiers had tried to tighten their encirclement but had been stopped, though I didn't learn how. I heard numerous stories that day in both the Provincial Capital building and in the streets about the military probing the city's perimeter and how they were moving ever closer. It was clear that the noose around the city was being tightened.

The Provincial Capital was humming with activity. To prepare for the inevitable military invasion, the leaders in the Provincial Capital and members of the citizens' militia were mobilizing and planning for their last stand. Jeeps and military trucks full of armed young men, some of whom were wearing captured riot police helmets or who had bandanas over their lower faces, were moving in and out of the complex. These were intended to be used as rapid response teams to counter probes by the military. I noticed an increase in their comings and goings throughout the day, but I may have been more acutely aware of their movements due to my discussions with people in the Provincial Capital.

Gloom was starting to hang over the city. As I walked around inside the Provincial Capital building, I could see that certain people had resigned themselves to the fact that the troops were going to attack soon. The looks on a lot of people's faces had changed and become stone-like. They knew what the future might hold for them, and that they had made what might be a final decision.

Just before noon, I met Tim and Judi in front of the Provincial Capital. They had just returned from meeting with the missionaries, who had been told that all foreigners should leave Kwangju. Tim, Judi, and the missionaries had all decided to stay in the city. Tim noted that the missionaries had offered us a place to stay on their compound should we desire, but we all decided to stay at Tim's to keep Sun-jae and his mother safe.

Throughout the day on Monday, we were approached by several journalists who asked if we could interpret for them. We split up to help them and made plans to meet at the memorial service in the afternoon. On and off throughout the day I worked with perhaps six journalists, who were usually in groups. One of these journalists was Henry Scott-

Stokes of *The New York Times*, who had just arrived in Kwangju. He told us he had heard that the Chun regime had wanted to bomb the city, but the U.S. government intervened to make sure that didn't happen. I took him into the Provincial Capital and to the Sangmugwan gymnasium to see the coffins laid out for the memorial service.

That afternoon, a joint memorial service was held for the fallen resting in Sangmugwan. Though we had taken several journalists there to see the coffins in the past two days, there weren't as many journalists at the memorial as I would have expected. There were only about 40 coffins in the gymnasium, which was less than half the number resting there two days earlier. When I asked some of the committee members about the reduced number of coffins, I was told that many families had already taken their loved ones away so they could hold private services. I was also told that there were still at least 20 coffins lined up outdoors next to the main Provincial Capital building that had not been claimed by families.

The memorial service, which was organized by the committee running the Provincial Capital to focus on those who had lost their lives, was very solemn and reminded everyone of the indiscriminate brutality the citizens of Kwangju had suffered. People gathered not only on the ground floor but also on the mezzanine that overlooked the gymnasium. Each coffin had family members keeping vigil over it. During the memorial ceremony, the names, ages, and occupations of the dead were shared with those in attendance.

Tim, Judi, and I watched the memorial with several journalists from the mezzanine. Tim did the bulk of the interpreting for them so they could understand what was being said during the memorial, and we both answered the reporters' questions when they sought clarification. Both before and after the service we walked among the coffins with the reporters and interpreted when asked. The reporters usually wanted to ask the family members about where and how the person died. What the reporters didn't know is that I usually apologized prior to asking the question and offered my condolences to the family members. They appreciated that and sometimes this would lead them to ask who I was, what I did, and where I was living, and then I would get around to the reporter's question. I think this helped the family members because it was such a painful time, and to intrude as the reporters did without seeming to understand the family's grief seemed quite rude to me. In many cases the families didn't really want to answer the reporter's questions, but they did want to talk about their loved ones.

Some of the grieving people I talked to asked us very telling questions: "Have these people died for nothing?" "Were their deaths in vain?" The somber proceedings ended with the singing of the national anthem.

After the memorial service ended, I returned to the Provincial Capital building. While I was there, it was clear that the people who had been trying to run and guard the city under great duress over the past few days were exhausted. Some of the people I spoke with said they had gone without sleep every night and had been lucky to get an hour of sleep during the day. They all assumed that the attack would occur early in the morning, before dawn, when people would be most tired. Several of these young men nodded off even as I was speaking with them.

A rally was held in the square in front of the Provincial Capital at 3 p.m., and though the square was crowded, the number of people present was less than previous days. There were more men than women in the crowd, and as always people seemed most interested in the progress of the negotiations with the military. The student committee discussed the untrustworthiness of the military when it came to the negotiations but did not publicly discuss how the military's encirclement of the city was tightening. I'm not sure why they didn't, but based upon my discussions with them, the people in the Provincial Capital were certain that Kwangju's citizens were not going to come to their aid when the military attacked. It was going to be up to them to provide a lasting memory of the stand that they had taken, and their reasons for doing so. To this end, a statement titled "Why were we forced to take up arms?" was printed and posted for people to read.

The statement first honored the "the citizens and students who sacrificed their lives while fighting and shedding blood to defend this region and democracy" and then asked, "Why were we forced to take up arms? The answer is so simple. You and I took up arms because we couldn't bear to see such cruel atrocities." It criticized the government for extending martial law after students promised to return to classes and for sending paratroopers to Kwangju to "commit unspeakably cruel and ruthless acts of brutality". In addition to this, "from the night of May 20, martial law authorities issued a firing order and began firing indiscriminately. Democratic citizens who gather here to protect this town! What can we do in such a situation? What should we do? I want to ask. We couldn't suffer any more. Therefore, to protect this place and to protect our parents, brothers and sisters, we each held guns in our hands." Asking for understanding, they promised to keep the city safe and return the guns if negotiations turned in the city's favor, and asked citizens to cooperate with the citizens' militia.

After the rally I went back to the Provincial Capital building and spoke with whomever had time to talk. Most of the time, and particularly that Monday, the people there were busy. The conversations I had in the afternoon and early evening, however, tended to be longer and more pointed, with the focus being on the need to get the truth out about what had happened in Kwangju. I was told in the late afternoon that students were sneaking out of the city to try to spread the word about what was happening. People hoped that by making the rest of the country aware, it would inspire people elsewhere to take to the streets.

Part of this strategy was rooted in the fact that people knew the military would soon attack. As the day wore on, I could see in the faces of the people in the Provincial Capital an increasing awareness that this could be their last day. In the afternoon and early evening, several people said farewell to me in a very final-sounding manner.

With the end drawing nearer, the student organizers attempted to talk to as many journalists as possible to make sure that their stance, their demands, and their points of view were recorded and conveyed to those outside of Kwangju. There seemed to be more requests that day for foreign journalists to reach out to the U.S. Embassy to explain what was happening and to urge the Embassy to help mediate a peaceful settlement.

Prior to Monday, a spokesperson designated by the student committee had spoken to reporters on behalf of the leadership in the Provincial Capital. Yun Sang-won had not spoken to the press because he had not wanted to take time away from his other duties, but now that he knew it was almost over, he decided to make himself available to the press more than once that afternoon.

One press conference was held in the meeting room where I had first met Yun. After the gathered reporters sat down around the table, Yun and the spokesperson spoke and answered questions. As Tim had the best Korean and presentation skills, he interpreted, and I helped out when needed. Speaking to the reporters, Yun stated that the military could not be trusted and reiterated his request for the American ambassador to mediate a peaceful settlement. In response to a question, he also stated that should the military attack, he and the others would fight to the end to defend the city.

The press conference ended, and the reporters filed out of the room. Yun thanked me and Tim for interpreting. Yun and I shook hands and said goodbye. It felt very final, because we both knew there was a good chance that we would not see each other again.

After the press conference I wandered around the Provincial Capital building and spoke with people I had met over the past two days. They all believed the military was going to attack that night. Many said their final goodbyes to me and asked me not to forget them. Since I had borne witness to what had happened in Kwangju, and inside the Provincial Capital, they made me promise that I would make sure the world learned the truth about what had happened.

I then met up with Henry Scott-Stokes, who had attended a separate press conference with Yun and written an article, which his colleagues had left the city to file. It was only much later that I found out he had reported Yun's request for mediation by the American ambassador. I walked with him to his inn, which was just off of Geumnam-ro. He told me he thought most of the Korean journalists working with the foreign reporters were reporting to the KCIA. From other conversations I had, it seemed many foreign journalists were suspicious of the Korean reporters and worried about the accuracy of their translations. We would sometimes be asked by a journalist if the translation they had been provided was correct. The translations they heard were often polished or sanitized and spun in a positive way, so we would often provide them with our own interpretation of what was said.

In the late afternoon, there was one last press conference held in the Provincial Capital building. It was led by the student spokesperson, who explained the student committee's position but also implored the reporters to do their jobs correctly and make sure the world knew what was happening in Kwangju.

After the press conference I tried to meet as many people as I could in the Provincial Capital building to say goodbye. They knew that tonight was potentially their last night, so I made it clear that I thought it was not a permanent farewell, but rather a "See you again soon." I wanted them to know that I was proud of them and that no matter what, we would meet again. In that moment, it was hard to maintain a positive expression on my face when we looked each other in the eye.

There was a finality to this day unlike any of the other days I had spent in the Provincial Capital. Running through my mind were worries about the final outcome, and how high the death toll might be. I could not figure out how I would be able to cope with it all. How do you deal with the possibility of a large number of people you know all dying in a short period of time?

I returned to Tim's and we had dinner around 7 p.m. After dinner we discussed what we thought might happen that night. Because we were all exhausted, we went to bed around 9 p.m. I fell asleep immediately; I don't know if it was due to exhaustion or if I was trying to escape from what I knew was coming.

12. Bearing Witness
Tuesday, May 27

We were awoken around 3:30 a.m. by the sound of a young woman's voice over a loudspeaker. She announced that the soldiers were coming, begged the citizens of Kwangju to come out to the Provincial Capital and defend their city, and implored them to never forget those making a final stand. From the sound of her voice, it sounded like she was on the move, so we assumed that she was being driven around in a jeep. To this day, I could swear that at one point I heard her speak in halting English for a few sentences, though this could have been my imagination.

Everyone in the house was awake by this point. Judi came into our room, while Sun-jae's mother remained in hers. We knew this was the end. We couldn't hear people leaving their houses and answering the woman's pleas, so we knew it would just be the people at the barricades and in the Provincial Capital who would put up resistance. Based upon my conversations with them, I knew they would resist until the end. Worried about the possibility of the military shooting toward the house, we took the mattresses and leaned them against the front wall. Sitting in the darkened room, our faces barely visible in the ambient light, we wondered how violent the fighting was going to be. We also talked about the possibility that we might be singled out in the aftermath.

I told Tim I thought I should head to the Provincial Capital building and sit in front of the gate, that maybe the presence of an American would stop the military from violently retaking the Provincial Capital. Tim talked me out of that idea. We heard shooting. The single shots of M-1s were followed by bursts of automatic gunfire. The only break in the ongoing and increasingly loud song of futility and desperation was the voice of that lone woman. It was painful to hear her increasingly desperate pleas for the citizens of Kwangju to come out and help defend the city interspersed with the sound of automatic gunfire. We heard her voice off and on for about 20 minutes before it went silent.

Later, around 4:30 a.m., we began to hear the rumbling of what sounded like tanks as they rolled down the streets near the house. Before long we heard soldiers in the street in front of the house. Tim and I wondered if they were going to enter the house or not, so we went out on the rooftop and poked our heads out cautiously to see what was going on in the street below. The sky was getting lighter by this point, so we could see the soldiers were going from house to house and searching for suspected militants. They were not targeting every house, however, so they seemed to know which ones to search. We could see they were wearing white armbands and white bands around their helmets, and realized they were likely not the dreaded black beret paratroopers, but regular army soldiers. This made us hopeful that there would be minimal violence elsewhere in the city.

Throughout this time we could hear the sound of shooting, of resistance to the military's invasion, particularly in the direction of the Provincial Capital. There was a clear difference in the sounds we could hear from the attackers and defenders. We heard the bursts of the soldiers' M-16s versus the small cracks of the M-1s used by the citizens' militia, which sounded so feeble in comparison. By 7 a.m., we could no longer hear any shots.

We gathered in the main room and Sun-jae's mother made us breakfast. Though I wasn't very hungry, I ate a little so as not to be rude. Since there was no longer any gunfire, I decided to go to the Provincial Capital to see what had happened. Tim and Judi were hesitant, but by that point I had come to accept that whatever will be, will be. If I was supposed to die, be shot, or be arrested, I could not worry about it because there were more important things at stake. I wanted to see how much bloodshed had occurred and to bear witness to the situation at the Provincial Capital before it was potentially covered up and sanitized. At around 8:30 a.m. or 9 a.m. I left the house and began walking slowly toward the Provincial Capital building. Tim and Judi quickly caught up with me.

When we left the house, the only people we saw in the streets were soldiers. They were standing or walking in pairs or larger groups, and we couldn't really walk anywhere without encountering them. Though they hadn't yet set up checkpoints, as we moved closer to the city center, we saw soldiers stopping, searching, and arresting people. Luckily, they didn't have any interest in us. We decided to stop and ask a soldier what was happening, and why they were in Kwangju. He said he had been told that they were there to put down a communist insurrection. We asked a number of soldiers the same question and always got the same answer.

In addition to the soldiers, their tanks and APCs, we encountered disturbing evidence of the fighting that had occurred. As we walked toward Geumnam-ro, we saw pools of blood on the sidewalk, and occasionally in the street as well. As we got closer to the Provincial Capital, we started to come across bodies. In some cases, there were single bodies and in others there were four or five bodies together. We could see from where blood pooled in the street that some of the dead had been moved by the soldiers onto the sidewalks. The soldiers left them lying there covered by woven rice straw bags that only hid their heads and upper bodies but left their feet and lower legs sticking out from underneath. By the time we reached the Provincial Capital, we had already counted fifteen bodies.

I kept silently hoping that the amount of bloodshed would not be as severe as it had been during the days before the citizens took over the city. It was like a mantra to ready myself for what we were about to see, because we had no idea what to expect. What would we find when we reached the Provincial Capital? Had the military left the bodies of the defenders in the street as an example, or had it dealt with them in a dignified manner? In light of the bodies we were finding in the streets, as well as those we had already seen in the hospitals and morgues, I was bracing myself for the worst.

As we approached the city center, we saw more tanks and APCs. We also saw soldiers marching citizens who had been arrested and tied together in a line, with their hands and arms tied behind their backs. The soldiers barked orders at them, kicked them, and hit them with rifle butts. We also saw soldiers bringing arrested people to collection points where they were forced to lie face down, and where they were subject to more hitting, kicking, and yelling.

When we reached the Provincial Capital, it was guarded by tanks and APCs with their guns trained on the roads that converged in front of it. The main building had been riddled with gunfire and there had clearly been a fire on the left side of the building. Smoke still hung in the air. At ground level, soldiers were standing behind the fence which ringed the complex, spaced about 10 to 12 feet[13] apart. We could also see soldiers on

---

[13] 10 feet to 12 feet is about 3 to 3.5 meters.

Bound students being marched away by soldiers after the capture of the city on May 27.

the roof and inside the main building; they were visible through the upper story windows, some of which were open, some of which had been shot out.

As I started to walk toward the Provincial Capital, Tim and Judi stopped and decided they wanted to go to the missionary compound first to see what had happened there. Intending to meet later, we parted.

I approached the main Provincial Capital building and walked around the outside of it to get a better look at the damage. As I did so, I noticed shell casings on the ground. There were lots of M-16 shell casings left by the soldiers, as well as some M-1 shell casings that had come from the defenders. I picked up a few M-16 casings and an M-1 casing and put them in my pocket, where they would stay for the next few days. Unlike other parts of the city, there were no pools of blood in the street outside of the Provincial Capital.

I walked up to one of the soldiers guarding the main gate to the Provincial Capital and asked him in Korean why the soldiers were there, and he gave the same reply as the others about a communist insurrection. The reason I kept asking this question to the soldiers I encountered was because a part of me thought that the military authorities had to have lied to the soldiers about what had been happening in Kwangju. For me, the only way it made sense for Koreans to think it was all right to attack other Koreans was because they believed they were facing communists or north Koreans. In response to his mention of a communist insurrection, I asked him if he was sure about this, and told him I had been in Kwangju since May 21 and had not met or heard about any communists or north Korean spies. I told him that the only people I had seenwere students and citizens, not communists. He listened, but I could see that he was becoming confused and starting to look around, clearly uncomfortable about the turn our conversation had taken.

Something else I remember was that the soldier didn't show any reaction when I began speaking to him in Korean, which I found a little odd at first. He did seem surprised when I told him I was an American and a Peace Corps Volunteer, however. After speaking further with him, I decided to see what I could get away with, and said, "I am going to walk around inside the Provincial Capital." I think this low-ranking soldier had no idea what to do with me, so he didn't try to stop me. Looking back on it, it was a little strange that I was able to get away with so much.

Inside the gate, smoke hung in the air. Mixed with the smell of burning wood was the smell of gunpowder, burnt flesh, and burnt hair. All around the front of the main building lay debris from the battle, a mixture of glass and stucco that had fallen from the places where the bullets had hit the outer walls of the building. Some of the bullet holes were larger than others, so in addition to M-16s the soldiers had clearly used larger-caliber guns. I walked around the building toward the courtyard in the back and saw soldiers guarding perhaps 15 prisoners, who were lying face-down on the ground. I quickly discovered there were limits to what I could get away with. The soldier nearest to me blocked my way and said in English, "No." When I asked him in Korean what was going on, he told me they were prisoners, and the area was off limits to civilians. I never found out whether the prisoners had been arrested in the Provincial Capital or if they had come from other places in the city.

I walked back around to the front of the building and went inside the main entrance. As I entered, I saw bullet holes in the walls. On the second floor, those in the walls facing the front of the building were high up, as if they had been fired from the ground outside the building. The bullet holes in the second floor's inner front walls, on the other hand, were at chest height, and had obviously been fired by soldiers on the second floor. It also appeared that a grenade had gone off. It soon became obvious that the military had not yet cleaned anything up and had left the dead where they fell. There were pools of blood, as well as smeared blood where it looked like a wounded person had crawled or been dragged away. As I walked farther into the building, I discovered one body after another. I couldn't bear the sight of it. They were all young, likely students. I didn't want to look close enough to see if I knew anyone. Some were not easy to identify. On the first floor I gasped as I recognized one of the dead as a person I had met in the building days earlier and hoped I wouldn't find anyone else.

When I went into the stairwell and began climbing the stairs, it was obvious there had been a fire there. As I reached the second floor, I saw a half-burnt body lying beneath a window. I recognized him as the student spokesperson who I had first met on Friday night when he had come to ask the journalists to contact the U.S. Embassy. As I moved about the second floor, I came across more bodies. Two lying near the spokesperson were people I had met previously. It was becoming too painful to take in.

I counted nine bodies, but I didn't get a chance to look around the entire building.

This was because shortly before 10 a.m. a soldier confronted me and told me I had to leave. I asked him what was happening, but he just told me I shouldn't have been let in. Once I was escorted out, I heard the loud sound an approaching helicopter. It landed in the square in front of the Provincial Capital, and out stepped an obviously high-ranking officer who was greeted with salutes by other officers. I spoke with one of the soldiers who was standing guard outside the complex and asked him what was happening. He told me that the officer who had arrived was the general in charge of the operation. I deduced that I had been asked to leave because the general was due to arrive, and the soldiers wanted to secure the perimeter. It became clear to me that the bodies had been left in place so the general could see for himself what had happened.

Since I couldn't go back in, I decided to walk around the outer fence of the Provincial Capital and then go see what was happening elsewhere. Walking in the direction of the YMCA and the stream that runs through downtown, I saw more pools of blood on the ground and bodies shrouded with woven rice bags.

I returned to the Provincial Capital around 11 a.m. to find the general gone. The prisoners I'd seen behind the complex were being taken away in large military trucks, while other prisoners were being marched into the complex from locations elsewhere in the city. I approached the gates and saw that foreign reporters had been let into the main building. Soldiers were bringing the bodies of the fallen out of the building one at a time and taking them around to the back of the building where the prisoners had been. I walked through the gates and into the Provincial Capital complex but soon turned around and walked out as it was just too much to deal with. I dreaded the thought of seeing more people I knew who had been cut down in the prime of their lives.

Out in the square, I ran into Tim and Judi, who seemed to have just arrived. We didn't say a lot to each other at first. Tim told me that while they were at the missionary compound, they had called the Peace Corps Office in Seoul. They were told the Peace Corps would pick us all up from the compound the next morning and take us to Seoul. The missionaries had again extended their offer to us to stay in the compound that night.

Tim finally asked, "Did you go inside?"

"Yes. It wasn't pretty," I answered. I couldn't say much more. When I tried to describe what I had seen, I was overcome by a flood of emotion and had to stop.

We soon saw some of the foreign reporters come out of the Provincial Capital and went to speak with them. They had watched the military attack the Provincial Capital from their hotel room. One of them, Terry Anderson, had tried to take a photo of the soldiers on the roof of the Provincial Capital building at the beginning of the attack. In response, a soldier had fired at them, causing them to drop to the floor and crawl hurriedly from the room. We followed them to their hotel room and listened to their vivid description of what had happened. They showed us the bullet holes, most of which were on the outer wall around the window, with a few in the room.

The journalists said they had been let into the Provincial Capital before I returned and had counted 17 bodies, but I couldn't be sure if we had counted the same bodies, since I had been forced to leave before I could look through the entire compound. After spending about an hour with them, I decided I wanted to see what was happening elsewhere in the city. Tim and Judi were a little hesitant to do this, so I went off by myself.

After I left, I wandered aimlessly around the city. I didn't think to eat lunch. In the early afternoon I saw someone I knew who had been involved in the uprising and approached him and asked if there was anything I could do to help. He was trying to make his way to a place where the soldiers wouldn't think to look for him, but he was afraid he would be stopped and arrested. I assumed that the military would not stop a Korean who was with an American, so I offered to walk with him. Despite there being groups of soldiers posted throughout the city, and despite us walking right in front of the Provincial Capital, no one ever said a word to us. Before long, I found other young men and citizens who needed help getting around the city and accompanied them as well.

Word spread quickly that there was a foreigner willing to escort people to safer locations, and soon I had mothers come up to me and request that I go to a certain address to find their son, asking, "Can you bring him to his aunt's house? He should be safer there." I was asked to take people who were trying to avoid being caught by the military to places they hadn't really been associated with, where they would be safer. I escorted one person at a time, being careful to make it seem like we were just out for a stroll and to not walk too quickly.

At one point when I returned to the Provincial Capital, I ran into some of the journalists. We talked for a bit, but I didn't mention anything about what I was up to because I was concerned that it could cause problems if it was reported. I spent the day escorting people around the city, and finished around 4 p.m., when I returned to Tim's place. I discovered Tim had been doing something similar, and I believe he was accompanied by Judi.

We talked more about the plans for the Peace Corps to pick us up the next day. Tim and Judi had decided to take the missionaries up on their offer to let us stay in an empty house in their compound. Considering the military's arrests of young people, Tim also wanted to bring Sun-jae to the compound so that he would be safe that night. The orders from the Peace Corps were to only bring essentials and not to bring anything related to the last ten days because the van might be stopped and searched. After eating a dinner cooked by Sun-jae's mother, we took Sun-jae with us to the compound. It was his first time outside in over a week.

Once we got to the compound and settled in, Tim and Sun-jae went for a walk outside to see what was happening and to talk and have a drink. Despite the risks, I think it relieved some of the tension.

That evening, Tim, Judi, and I stayed up and wrote down what we had experienced over the past ten days. It was a stressful night, not only because we were forced to relive the events of the uprising, but also because there were rumors the military might search the houses in the compound because it was known that many people had taken refuge with the missionaries. Luckily, this didn't happen. As with every other night that week, by the time we went to sleep I was exhausted.

13. Consequences

Wednesday, May 28 to Monday, June 2

Wednesday, May 28

We woke up early. There was some food in the house, but while the others helped themselves to eggs and cereal, I just had coffee. Sun-jae's mother had asked that we bring her son home before we left Kwangju, since she felt she could protect him best there, so Tim walked him home. Before he left, I gave him my thanks for letting us stay at his house and asked him to say goodbye to his mother and to stay safe. Tim escorted him home, and then returned to the compound.

Around 10:30 a.m. a van pulled up outside the house. Inside was a Korean driver and an American Peace Corps official. The official reiterated that we were not to bring anything pertaining to the last ten days, an order Tim and I ignored. Tim was carrying the accounts of what we had seen and a copy of the "Why We Took Up Arms" statement. In my bag was a roll of undeveloped film and the shell casings I had picked up in front of the Provincial Capital building the previous morning. We got into the van and began what we assumed was a direct trip to Seoul. However, while we were heading toward the expressway, the van suddenly turned in another direction, leading Tim and I to look at each other and wonder, "Where are we going?" We drove into a neighborhood on the outskirts of Kwangju where we stopped in front of a house. We were surprised to see another PCV get into the van. She told us she had been there the entire time and that she had called the Peace Corps office in Seoul early on and had been told to stay indoors. She said her homestay family had refused to let her go out.

The trip to Seoul took about five hours, but it went by in a blur because I was trying to process everything that had happened. We were told that James Mayer, the Peace Corps Director for Korea, wanted to speak to us all. We wondered if we might be sent home. We arrived around 4 p.m. and were dropped off in front of the Peace Corps building and told to go upstairs. We were led to a conference room where we were met by Director Mayer. In a fatherly fashion, he told us that we should have listened to the Embassy and left when we were told to. He then said he wanted to meet with all of us one by one. We were told to remain in the conference room and not to talk to any other PCVs who were in the office. If I remember correctly, I was the first person to meet with him alone. I followed him to his office.

He closed the door and had me sit down. After inquiring to see if I was all right, he asked me directly, "Did you spend the night in the Provincial Capital building?"

"Yes, I did," I said. I had no intention of lying because I knew what I had done was right and I did not feel that it had violated my affirmation of the Peace Corps oath. He disagreed. He told me that my actions in Kwangju violated the policies of the Peace Corps and that I had to resign from the Peace Corps that day. He told me I could either write the letter of resignation myself, or he would write the letter for me. He also told me that if he wrote it, I could either sign the letter or he would sign it for me. Whatever I chose, I was told, I was no longer a Peace Corps Volunteer. He then told me to take some time to think about whether I would write the letter, but I quickly gave him an answer. I told him I wouldn't write it because I didn't feel that I had done anything wrong. He told me he would write it and sent me back to the conference room.

When I got to the conference room, I told the others I was being forced out of the Peace Corps. Tim couldn't believe it. He didn't think that our actions in Kwangju had anything to do with politics and had instead been about helping people. I waited as they each met with the director. They were all allowed to remain in the Peace Corps. I was called into the Director's office again and presented with the letter to sign. Being the naïve 24-year-old that I was, I signed it, mostly because I had no recourse if I refused.

The Director then told me that the Korean government knew everything I had done in Kwangju, and that the Peace Corps and the U.S. Embassy could no longer guarantee my safety because the Korean government had implied it might be looking to do me harm. I found this hard to believe. In fact, I laughed when I recounted his words to Tim afterward. "There's no way they're going to harm me," I said. We hadn't done enough for anyone to worry about us. All we did was try to help journalists understand what had happened and try to ensure the injured were taken care of. On top of that, why would they target an American? It seemed to me to be a scare tactic to convince me to leave the country as quickly as possible.

With my letter of resignation signed, Director Mayer told me that I needed to go back down to Yeongam to get my things and I also needed to get a new passport, since the one I had been issued was for Peace Corps use only. He asked if I wanted money for a plane ticket, or if I wanted the Peace Corps to buy me the ticket. I asked for the money because I wanted to find a way to stay in Korea. I saw no reason to leave, and I was still concerned about what had happened in Kwangju. I felt that to leave would be to take the easy way out, and I knew there were a lot of people in Kwangju who had no way out.

The PCV who had stayed indoors in Kwangju left to stay at an inn near the Peace Corps office. Director Mayer told the rest of us that we could spend the night at his house, which was near Yonsei University. It was nice to have a place to stay, but it also ensured we would have minimal contact with other PCVs. Tim and I were led to one room, and Judi to another. Once we were in our room, Tim and I began to discuss what we were going to do next. He reached into his bag and pulled out the accounts we had written of what we had each seen in Kwangju.

"We've got to get our information in front of the U.S. government," I said. We decided that we had to go see the ambassador. We were upset by the lack of response by the United States and were certain our government would be appalled by the atrocities we had witnessed. That evening we discussed what should be included in, and omitted from, our description of events. We weighed what repercussions might arise if certain pieces of information were shared. To be honest, we weren't sure who to trust. Since my handwriting is difficult to read, Tim did most of the writing that night, and once we were finished, we went to sleep.

Thursday, May 29

The next morning, Tim, Judi, and I decided not to stay at the director's house another night. Instead, we went to Gwanghwamun and got rooms at an inn behind the Peace Corps office. In the early afternoon, Tim and I walked over to the U.S. Embassy with our eyewitness account. After we passed the marines guarding the front entrance, a friendly marine at the security desk on the ground floor stopped us and asked us what we wanted. After we explained why we were there, he made a call upstairs. Five minutes later an Embassy employee appeared. We explained who we were and said that we wanted to provide the Embassy with our written account and discuss it with the ambassador. He told us that the ambassador did not have time to talk to us and that the Embassy already knew everything that had happened in Kwangju, so we couldn't tell them anything they didn't already know. After telling us our help wasn't needed, he turned to go upstairs. We asked him to take our accounts and share them with the ambassador. He said he wouldn't, but we placed them in his hand anyway. He then went back upstairs, and we left.

Though we had been told to keep quiet about what had happened in Kwangju, over the next few days we talked to many other PCVs who were curious to hear what we had lived through. Word traveled quickly in the Peace Corps, and the fact that a handful of PCVs had refused to leave Kwangju quickly became common knowledge. Since there were so few of us there, people quickly figured out who had stayed. Since I was no longer a PCV, I felt particularly free to talk about these things. We met other PCVs at tearooms to talk over coffee or headed to bars to share what we'd seen over a few beers.

Friday, May 30

On Friday I went to a pay phone and used the business card Henry Scott-Stokes had given me to call him to let him know what had happened to me. I met him at the Chosun Hotel, and we spoke over coffee. He wasn't really surprised that we would be terminated for our actions, but he raised an eyebrow when I told him that I was the only one to be forced out. He thought either all of us or none of us would be punished.

It soon became clear that there were others who wanted to hear our story. On Friday I was in the yard at the inn where we were staying when I was told there was a phone call for me. It was from an American missionary who had heard from a PCV that we had remained in Kwangju, and that I had been forced out of the Peace Corps. She had also learned where we were staying. I was amazed she was able to find me, but it showed just how quickly news traveled and how resourceful people can be. She wanted to find out what had happened in Kwangju, so we arranged to meet later that day at a tearoom. It was there that I met Sue Rice, who was a member of what was known as the Monday Night Group. This was a group of foreign missionaries who had worked with dissidents throughout the 1970s, shared news about the repression under Park Chung-hee's dictatorship, and sent information out of the country to allies in the United States. She and her husband Randy were very active in the workers' rights movement in Incheon and Seoul.

Sue was a psychiatrist, and she told me she had been worried about our mental health, so she had contacted the Peace Corps and the U.S. Embassy to offer her services. She told them she was aware that PCVs had remained in Kwangju and, worried that we might have been traumatized by the experience, she offered her services to help us deal with what we had seen and experienced in Kwangju. The Peace Corps never mentioned this, however, and she told me that both the Peace Corps and the U.S. Embassy turned down her offer.

To find me, Sue had reached out using her impressive information network. She found out from a fellow PCV where I was staying and, hoping to catch me there, called the inn. After our initial meeting, I agreed to meet with her and her husband a few days later.

In between meetings like these I wandered around the city and tried to straighten out my thoughts and figure out my next move. In this I was helped by Bohdan. I received a message that he had tried to contact me, so I called him in Waegwan. As it turned out, he had heard during the uprising that PCVs had refused to leave Kwangju and assumed Tim and I were among those who had stayed. He had been so worried about our safety that he had considered trying to make his way there.

Bohdan had also heard through the grapevine that I had been forced out of the Peace Corps, which was the main reason he wanted to talk to me. He had been working for the past year for the University of Maryland teaching remedial reading and math to soldiers at Camp Carroll in Waegwan, and a job opening had just appeared. When he learned I was suddenly unemployed, he put in a good word for me with his superiors and arranged for me to work there. All I had to do was visit the university administrators at the main branch of the university on Yongsan Garrison to fill out the necessary paperwork. It remained to be seen, however, whether the Korean government would issue me a visa.

Saturday, May 31 to Monday, June 2

On Saturday night I went to Itaewon with Tim and a bunch of other PCVs. Starting out at a place with an excellent sound system, we made our way to a bar across from the Hamilton Hotel and drank rather heavily. As curfew approached, Tim and I decided to stay at a nearby inn. We were slow to finish up, so shortly after curfew had begun, Tim and I walked through the streets of Itaewon chanting the protest songs we had heard in Kwangju. Considering they had lyrics such as "Kim Dae-jung should be released" and "Chun Doo-hwan should resign," we received some really strange looks from Koreans. Luckily, we didn't have far to walk, and the police decided to just ignore the obviously drunk foreigners. Looking back, it might not have been the brightest idea, but it sure felt good. In fact, this was not the last time Tim and I would do that in Seoul.

During our stay in Seoul, Judi, Tim, and I spent a lot of time together because we had all shared similar experiences that helped form a bond between us. We were able to be together without feeling overwhelmed because we could guess how the other person was feeling. On Monday, June 2, Judi and Tim left Seoul and returned to Kwangju. It wasn't easy seeing them go, especially since I wasn't sure if I would be able to stay in Korea. Before they left, Tim and I exchanged contact information so I could keep him updated on my circumstances. We parted with the hope we would see each other soon.

Part III

Life after Kwangju

14. Finding and Defining

June to August 1980

On June 2, after Tim and Judi left, I met with Sue and Randy Rice and told them about what I had seen in Kwangju. They wanted to find out the truth of what had happened to disseminate this information among dissidents, missionaries, and other activists in Korea. Although Sue never offered me any counseling sessions, I think she decided that giving me the opportunity to share my experiences, and allowing me to talk about them, would be beneficial and would help me deal with what had happened. In the months to come, she and Randy would also offer me their home as a safe place to stay whenever I visited Seoul.

As it turned out, I would have good reason to visit. At our meeting, I mentioned that I had found a job teaching on base at Camp Carroll. When they realized this would give me access to the Army Post Office (APO), which was not subject to scrutiny by the Korean government, Sue asked me, "Would you be willing to use the APO connection to the United States to send and receive dissident material?" "Of course," I said, "I'd be happy to help that way." Faye Moon, another American member of the Monday Night Group, was about to return to the United States, so I was to take over her role in facilitating the dissident information pipeline. Faye had spent almost 20 years in Korea with her husband Stephen (Dong-hwan) Moon, who was the brother of pastor-activist Moon Ik-hwan,

The next day, I went to Yongsan Garrison to fill out the paperwork for my new job. I met Sue and Randy in the afternoon, and we had dinner together. Considering what I had seen in Kwangju and the fact I was no longer in the Peace Corps, Sue warned me that I was likely going to have someone following me. She and Randy were aware of this practice, since they were followed as well, and they also knew certain people were acting as informants. "You'll be able to tell because they won't try to hide it from you," she said. The point was to intimidate me.

The next day, Wednesday, I went to the U.S. Embassy to get a new passport since the one I had been issued before leaving for Korea was semi-diplomatic, as it was put to us, and for use by PCVs only. I was afraid I might be denied a new passport and forced to leave Korea. Luckily, I received a new one that day without any problems.

The next possible obstacle to staying in Korea was that the Korean government might deny me a visa. Fortunately, I chose a good time to go to the immigration office. I arrived at lunch time when there was only one clerk in the office. When I walked in, I could see that he was nervous about having to speak English, so when I spoke to him in Korean he burst into a smile. I explained that I was a former PCV with a new passport who wanted to stay in Korea. This was not very common at the time, so he happily gave me a two-year work visa without bothering to see if I was blacklisted. I was in and out in ten minutes. Despite my worries, everything went smoothly and by 1 p.m. I had a new passport and visa.

The next thing I needed to do was gather my things in Yeongam. That afternoon I took a bus to Kwangju. When I arrived, I went for a walk around the city. While the streets were full of people again, the atmosphere was tense, and everyone was being very careful. As I was walking in front of the Provincial Tuberculosis Control Headquarters, I crossed paths with one of the student leaders I had met during the uprising. We both recognized each other but knew we couldn't acknowledge this fact, so we made eye contact without turning our heads. I had to do this because, from what Sue and Randy had told me, I assumed I was being followed. I knew I had to cut off all contact with people I had known in Kwangju before and during the uprising because being seen with them could potentially put them in danger.

After spending the night in Kwangju, I went down to Yeongam to pack my bags and say goodbye to everyone at the health center. My departure was sudden for all of us. The Peace Corps had phoned ahead to tell them that my service was ending sooner than expected because I had to go back to the United States. I told them the real reason I had to leave the Peace Corps—that I had refused to leave Kwangju. The nurses, who had always acted like my older sisters, were all very concerned for me. Several of them wondered if I was crazy, and asked "What were you thinking, staying in Kwangju?" The men did not address what had happened and were very stoic about it all. Months later I wrote a letter in Korean to one of my co-workers to further explain why I had been forced out. His son wrote me back and said, "My father is very upset with you for what you did." I want to believe that this was out of concern for my safety, and that he was upset that I had put myself in harm's way. In a good illustration of how times change, when I met him again in 2010, he was proud of the fact that I had refused to leave Kwangju, and that my experiences there, and in Yeongam, had shaped the person I had become.

I went home and packed up my things, and then went to the post office. The staff there knew me and they helped me mail some boxes home to the United States. I also mailed two duffel bags to Waegwan, which arrived about a week later. I left a lot of stuff at my place in Yeongam and told the owner that she could do what she liked with it. After spending one last night in Yeongam, I took several buses to get to Waegwan, where I arrived Friday afternoon. I stayed with Bohdan and shared with him and his wife my experiences of the past few weeks. They were quite concerned about my health and how I was doing.

The next day, Steve and Carolyn, two K-45 PCVs, came to visit. We had gotten to know each other during training and had met up in Seoul from time to time over the previous two years. They were based near Daegu. They had heard I had been in Kwangju and forced out of the Peace Corps, and wanted to hear firsthand what had happened. I talked to them at length about what I had seen. Floored by what they heard, they told me they were leaving the country in a few days and wanted to know if they could help get the story out. I mentioned that I had taken about 36 photos during the uprising and smuggled the film out of Kwangju when we left. Steve and Carolyn offered to take the photos out of the country and to share them abroad.

I wanted to have the film developed prior to handing the negatives over to Steve and Carolyn, but I knew we couldn't use any Korean commercial photo services to develop the film because they would turn anything suspicious over to the KCIA. Luckily, one of Bohdan's hobbies was photography and he had access to a darkroom on base. I asked him if he could develop them for me, since he knew what he was doing. He agreed to develop the film, but unfortunately over half of the roll didn't develop properly. Nonetheless, several worthwhile photos turned out.

While this plan was unfolding, Carolyn and Steve took me to meet Sebastian Heinrich Rothler, whom they knew quite well. He was a German priest who had served as a missionary for 15 years at Waegwan Abbey. He was involved in dissident activity and even hid people who were on the run. He had also secretly published banned Korean books that were critical of Park Chung-hee. He gave me a couple of these books and, warning me it was illegal to have them, told me I could share them with any close friends who might be interested. It was likely through him that Steve and Carolyn received accounts of what had happened in Kwangju written by Korean Catholic priests. I would meet with him a few more times during my time in Waegwan. As it turned out, he was also connected with the Rices and the Monday Night Group.

Steve and Carolyn stayed the night and returned home Sunday with my written account and the negatives. They left the country on June 10, and so began the photos' journey around the world. They first flew to Tokyo and tried sharing them with different groups there but found it hard to make any headway. They then went to Stockholm, where, using pseudonyms, they gave interviews to journalists about the atrocities PCVs had witnessed in Kwangju. As a result, Agence France-Presse (AFP) and the Swedish newspaper *Dagens Nyheter* published articles about them on July 15, and the Associated Press followed with two articles on July 20 and 22.

In response to the articles, the South Korean Embassy in Stockholm tried to locate them, and we know now that the Korean foreign ministry contacted the U.S. Embassy in Seoul on July 19 to state that it was "very disturbed" by their statements attesting to the high number of deaths in Kwangju. Korea's foreign ministry asked the U.S. government to contact AFP to correct the record, but the Embassy declined to do this, though it did confirm that Steve and Carolyn had previously been PCVs in Korea. Steve and Carolyn eventually returned to the United States and contacted a journalist at the *Milwaukee Journal*, which published an article titled "Trio dispute death toll in Korean strife" on August 12, 1980. The journalist phoned me in Waegwan to ask me questions. Steven and Carolyn also wrote articles for the December 1980 issue of a magazine called *Covert Action Information Bulletin*, which published several of the photos I had taken.

The Korean government attempted to control the narrative about what had happened in Kwangju in other ways. Tim, who wanted to remain in Korea, extended his service with the Peace Corps for another year and returned to the United States for a visit during the summer. When he returned to Korea in August 1980, we met in Seoul and he told me that Korean government officials had shown up at his parents' house in Minnesota and told them, "You need to make sure your son stays quiet." They also pressured Tim by contacting his home-stay mother and reminding her that her son was about to start his mandatory military service, implying that something could happen to him if Tim spoke out.

15. Waegwan, Seoul, and Dissidents

September 1980 to July 1981

W hile all of this was happening, I was settling into life in Waegwan. Bohdan arranged for me to move into a room in the same boarding house where he and his wife Yeong-suk were living. Rather than having meals provided, Yeong-suk cooked for us. The boarding house was about a 15-minute walk from Camp Carroll, near the center of town but outside the "ville," the neighborhood of stores and bars that catered to soldiers.

I worked on base for the University of Maryland teaching remedial reading and math to U.S. military personnel. I also taught American culture to KATUSAs, or Korean soldiers who served in the U.S. Army. I met some interesting people in the classroom. The KATUSAs were always well-behaved, which wasn't always true of the American soldiers. Some of them just goofed off, but there were a lot of good people who were trying to get ahead in their lives. The most impressive student I taught was also the only one who had any interest in Korea. Most soldiers never left the "ville," but this young man, who hadn't graduated high school but was very smart, had married a Korean woman and was living with her in a small village. He spoke Korean fluently. He wanted to get his GED and then take college courses; I told him, "If you can learn Korean, then you're already ahead of everyone else. You'll be able to do whatever you want." With students like him, teaching could be rewarding, but the hours were often long and tiring.

While I was in Waegwan I was able to confirm that I was being followed by a detective. I liked to go for walks out in the rice paddies, so it was easy to spot him tailing me. He also talked to our landlord. I think he was most interested in the people I was meeting because the government was still looking for people who had escaped Kwangju. I got pretty used to him being around, but never did what some of the Korean dissidents did, which was to buy the agent lunch from time to time!

The authorities likely had good reason to keep an eye on me, considering that I had become a participant in the dissidents' information pipeline. I went up to Seoul about once a month, and because Sue and Randy gave me a place to stay, I spent a lot of time interacting with the missionaries. Drawing on a variety of sources, they would fill me in on what was going on not only in Seoul but throughout the country. I was often given packets to take with me so I could mail them to the U.S., though sometimes they gave such materials to other visitors who were about to leave the country. I usually mailed or received information packets once or twice a month. The material being sent was about Kwangju or human rights violations and was selected by missionaries such as Faye Moon and Sue Rice, or by dissidents' wives who had information they wanted to get out of Korea. I usually mailed the packets to Korean pro-democracy, anti-dictatorship groups in Washington, D.C., or, after Faye Moon returned to the United States, to her home in New York State.

Since any foreign news reports that were critical of the Korean government were censored or banned, they also wanted me to help bring into Korea uncensored versions of these magazine articles and reports. When I received these, I would bring them with me on my next visit to Seoul and pick up the next packet. Trusting that being American would protect me from being searched, I didn't really try to hide these materials other than to stuff them in my backpack with other papers. Though the agent following me must have known what I was up to, he never intervened in any way.

One of the most interesting places I visited during my trips to Seoul was Galilee Church, which many wives and mothers of imprisoned dissidents attended. Sue Rice took me there for the first time in October 1980, and I went two more times after that. Since the church was for women, and the male missionaries didn't go, I was the only man there. I was glad I went because it was amazing. That was when I realized the women of Korea were its true strength, and I could see how foolish the Korean government was not to realize these women were keeping the movement going while their husbands were in prison. They were remarkable, and when I met them decades later, if I mentioned Galilee Church, it would bring tears to their eyes.

When I attended a prayer meeting there in December 1980, I was invited to take part in a memorable party held by Park Yong-gil, the wife of Moon Ik-hwan. Moon was then in prison, one of the many dissidents arrested on May 17. Park, like most dissident women, knew who the detective following her was and generously tried to make his life easier by doing things such as telling him where she was going, offering him food, or even inviting him to come in out of the rain. Her detective had reciprocated her kindness by giving her a Christmas cake, so the afternoon was spent eating it while her two-year-old grandson entertained us by telling us that he thought Chun Doo-hwan was "shit." The poet Kim Chi-ha's mother, who was also present, told us that her son had been released unexpectedly. This was a bit of good news at a time when it was in short supply, particularly considering that Kim Dae-jung had recently been sentenced to death, and the dissident leaders had been moved from prisons in or near Seoul to separate prisons around the country to make visiting them more difficult, and to keep the prisoners from coordinating hunger strikes.

The weekend after that, I went to Kwangju for the third time since the uprising. Although the atmosphere was better than during my previous visit in September, it was still tense. During the five or so times I visited Kwangju after 5.18, I often met Tim, but sometimes I just wandered around the city by myself as I tried to sort out in my head what had happened there the previous May. During my visit in January, I confirmed that the office of the U.S. Information Service had been burned down before Christmas. I soon learned from Sue Rice that five students had been arrested for arson, and that at least 300 KCIA agents were at Chonnam University, with two openly placed in each class to intimidate the students.

I also experienced this government-sponsored paranoia closer to home. Bohdan was teaching his wife Yeong-suk photography, so one morning she went out to the market to take photos. That afternoon, the police came to our boarding house and asked our landlord where the "spy" was because they had received a report that a woman who lived there was in the market taking photos. Since they thought she was photographing "bad things" that exposed poverty, they believed she could be a spy who would sell the pictures to north Korea. Luckily, our landlord was a former police officer who assured his visitor that the report was nonsense, but it brought home the claustrophobic paranoia of the time.

I told stories like this to my parents in the weekly letters I wrote them. They had been annoyed by the Peace Corps back in May when they got no information about my whereabouts except for a call on May 29 during which they were told that I had been safely removed from Kwangju, but nothing more. They understood my decision to stay, and my subsequent involvement with the missionaries, because it fit well with my Quaker upbringing. Since mail sent through the APO wasn't monitored by the Korean government, I could talk openly about Kim Dae-jung's sham of a trial and his death sentence and discuss the urgent need for pressure against the Korean government and our own. In response, my mother wrote letters to the editor of our local newspaper, made sure that our local Quaker meeting knew what was happening in Korea, and communicated with the American Friends Service Committee. In 1979 this Philadelphia-based group had started publishing a newsletter called the Korea Report, which was edited by David and Maude Easter, who were former PCVs. It focused on both the human rights situation in Korea and the role the United States played in supporting Chun Doo-hwan.

In early February 1981, Chun Doo-hwan was invited to the White House by the recently inaugurated President Reagan. In response, Chun commuted Kim Dae-jung's death sentence to life in prison. Chun got as much mileage as he could out of his visit to Washington. I learned from the missionaries that Korean-Americans in Washington were forced to come out and cheer his arrival. Their relatives in Korea were threatened and told that they would be fired from their jobs, and photos were taken to make sure they were present and cheering.

As these events were unfolding, I decided to return to the United States to pursue a Ph.D. in either microbiology or neurobiology. I had long been interested in science, particularly microbiology, and had even won my sixth-grade science fair with a project titled "Why Must We Wash Our Hands." My work at the Yeongam Health Center had deepened this interest. I had learned from my experiences as a tuberculosis caseworker that infectious diseases were a large-scale problem, as well as an area in which many people around the world could be helped. And while my time at the health center in Yeongam had taught me that diagnostics are a key foundation for good healthcare, it also made clear that there were many gaps in our knowledge that needed to be filled. On top of this, my experience during the Kwangju Uprising, when I had seen so many people willing to sacrifice themselves for others, had opened my eyes and taught me that I shouldn't focus on myself, but rather on people who are marginalized and those who could benefit the most from my help. Pursuing a Ph.D. in microbiology, a topic I naturally gravitated toward, would allow me to work to improve the lives of as many people as possible.

Using the resources available at Camp Carroll, such as information about universities on microfiche in the library, I began the application process in late 1980. Being overseas made the process slower and more complicated, but at least I could use the APO to send away for catalogues and information about programs and professors I might want to work with. My parents also helped arrange to have transcripts sent to me, and with their help I applied to ten different Ph.D. programs. I assumed that if I was accepted I would have to leave Korea in June to start orientation in July.

As time went on, teaching on the military base became a bit of a grind, particularly when I had students with discipline problems. As I put it to my parents in a letter, "I wish I had a job in 'Korea,' but then there would be no APO which everyone relies on. I must try and find someone to take over when I leave."

I continued working at Camp Carroll until March 1981, when I was told the second teaching position was being eliminated. Though I wasn't happy to move away from Bohdan, I chose to be transferred to Busan. I moved there at the end of March and settled into a room in the bachelor officer quarters at Camp Hialeah. Some of the officers were friendly and invited me out for drinks. I had been teaching there for two weeks when I got a phone call from the University of Maryland head office in Seoul telling me to pack up everything and come to Seoul because I was being terminated. I was not given a reason. I did as I was told, and when I met the head of the program in Seoul, he told me that I was reported to have said to the officers I went out drinking with that the only reason I was working at that job was to be able to use the APO system to move documents in and out of the country. Since I had never said anything like that to anyone on base, I surmised that a search of my mail at Camp Carroll had turned up dissident documents and I was moved to Busan to isolate me from Bohdan, which would make it easier to fire me.

With the job at the University of Maryland terminated, I moved into an inn near the Peace Corps office and contacted a former PCV I knew who was teaching English in Seoul. I had met Bruce Fulton, who is now a well-known professor and translator, when he was still a PCV. He had stayed in Korea after his service and gotten a job teaching English, and I knew he was using his position to help former PCVs secure jobs as English teachers. He was great that way and was always taking care of others.

He found me a job teaching English to corporate employees, particularly those working for corporations that had operations in the Middle East. I taught classes in the morning and afternoon in company seminar rooms. I taught in places such as the Daewoo Building across from Seoul Station and other corporate headquarters in Jongno. The classes were anywhere from one to three hours long and were intended to prepare the employees to be able to function while doing construction projects in the Middle East. The classes I taught always had more men than women, though one class at Daewoo had a few young women who were headed to the Middle East to be office workers.

I usually enjoyed teaching these classes, though I never found teaching English to be very exciting. Some days I had students who didn't really want to learn, a problem I had encountered while teaching on the military base. But overall, I taught some very interesting people, including a former government official who was going to the Wharton School of the University of Pennsylvania for a year to teach.

In mid-April I was invited by Sue Rice to a gathering to celebrate the 70th wedding anniversary of Moon Jae-rin and Kim Sin-muk, the parents of Moon Ik-hwan and Moon Dong-hwan. The event, held in Seoul, was also intended to show support for Moon Ik-hwan, who was on hunger strike in prison at the time, and there I met his son, Moon Sung-keun, who later became an actor. I really liked the Moon family. Moon Jae-rin was very friendly and mild-mannered. After the ceremony there was a picnic for a small group of people that Sue and I were lucky enough to be invited to. There I was able to meet many of the wives and mothers of dissidents, which reinforced in my mind the power of the women involved in the democracy movement. I was in awe of them all because I knew what they had been through.

Since I was living in Seoul, I was also able to attend the Quaker meetings at Ham Seok-heon's house regularly. Some Sundays he went to Busan to attend meetings there, but when he was present for the meetings in Seoul there were always more people in attendance. After worship, a small group of people would gather around him to hear what he had to say. I took part as well and listened to him, comprehending bits and pieces. Whenever Teacher Ham was present, I always felt like I was in the presence of someone very special, someone I wanted to learn from. My experiences listening to Teacher Ham, speaking with the wives and mothers of dissidents, and befriending those who were willing to sacrifice themselves in Kwangju revealed to me my life's path. These extraordinary people allowed me to learn from their experiences and showed me how to find the wisdom and commonality of all religious teachings and beliefs and adapt them to everyday life. It is an approach to life which has allowed me to accept my path but, more importantly, to put others before myself, to treat people with kindness, and to always remember the importance of empowering people.

In June 1981 I was contacted by Faye Moon, who by that time had moved to the United States. She discovered that the International Human Rights Law Group, which was based in Washington, D.C., was petitioning the United Nations Commission on Human Rights (UNCHR) regarding human rights violations in Korea. She had them reach out to me for help with their petition so I wrote a description of what happened in Kwangju based upon the notes I had. I gave my handwritten account to the Rices and they had it sent securely to the U.S., where it was typed, notarized, and included in the petition.

As June turned to July, I was still teaching English and had not received any news about my Ph.D. applications. On July 4 I made a collect call to my parents from Gwanghwamun Post Office, where many PCVs made calls home. During our conversation my parents told me I had been accepted into a doctorate program to study microbiology and immunology at Temple University Medical School in Philadelphia. "Oh," they added, "You need to start on the first of August."

In response to this news, I had to scramble to book a flight home, say goodbye to friends, and pack everything up. It was even more hectic because I decided to keep teaching until only a few days before I left. I had limited time for goodbyes, but by that time Bohdan had already left Korea to attend graduate school in the United States. I didn't have time to go see Tim but sent him a short letter with my contact information. My final goodbyes were with Sue and Randy Rice, who had been there for me in the year since 5.18. They gave me contact information for activists they knew in the United States so I could continue my involvement with Korea.

On July 25, 1981, I took a bus to Gimpo Airport, checked in my large backpack stuffed with clothes and camping equipment, and then headed for passport control. At the desk were an immigration official and a soldier. I was glad they chose not to inspect my carry-on bag, since I was carrying a large amount of dissident material that would have been confiscated, and I probably would have been held for questioning. The soldier asked if I would be returning to Korea soon. I told him I was going back to the United States to go to school. He then told me it was a good thing I was not planning to return, since my name was on the blacklist of people not allowed into the country.

What should have been uneventful flights to Philadelphia via Narita, Seattle, and Minneapolis, became more interesting when I arrived in Seattle to find that no bags had been placed on the flight at Gimpo. No one knew why. Our late arrival, and my wait for my bag, resulted in me having to make a dash across the airport to reach my plane to Philadelphia, which I climbed aboard just before they closed the door. After that exhausting struggle, I sank into my seat and slept most of the way home.

16. Trying to Stay True
1981 to present

Less than a week after I returned home, I started a new chapter as a graduate student. Adjusting to this new experience presented certain challenges, particularly since I'd barely had time to get used to being back in the United States. In addition to this, English had become something of a second language to me. When I started my studies, I still thought mostly in Korean, so I had to translate the Korean in my head back into English. There were times that I didn't realize that people were speaking to me because they hadn't used my Korean name. As a result, I initially felt out of place and out of sync with others. More than three years had passed since I had last studied. I was anxious that I was not as smart as everyone else, so I compensated for this by working twice as hard as my classmates. There were times when I wanted to drop out, but my memories of what I had seen in Kwangju convinced me not to give up. The example I had seen there of people willing to selflessly sacrifice for a greater goal provided a constant reminder to look beyond my immediate struggles and focus on my long-term objective, which was to put myself in a position where I could help as many people as possible.

Though I was busy with graduate school, I remained involved in the movement for human rights and democracy in Korea. In fact, waiting for me when I got home from Korea was a letter from the International Human Rights Law Group with a copy of their petition to the UNCHR. In it they thanked me for my contribution, particularly because "eyewitness testimony is very difficult to obtain."

After starting graduate school, I joined a Korean Human Rights group which met monthly at the Quaker Friends Center in Philadelphia. Our meetings focused on human rights in both north and south Korea, and covered topics such as Kwangju and the exploitation of Korean workers by American and Korean firms. The group belonged to the greater Peace Network which brought to light human rights violations around the world and took part in global efforts to achieve peace, which included a focus on the divided Koreas. We occasionally hosted guest speakers, including some from Korea.

I also kept in touch with the missionaries I had met in Korea. Faye Moon, for example, had left Korea before me, and her house in New York state was one of the addresses I mailed dissident material to when I had APO access. Though I only saw her once at a meeting on Korean human rights, we stayed in touch via occasional letters. I also corresponded with Jean Basinger, another member of the Monday Night Group who I'd met in Seoul shortly before her move back to the United States. We were both part of a Korean human rights network, but never crossed paths since she lived in Iowa. The Korean human rights groups were organized locally, and information was shared between the different groups within the United States as well as with groups in Japan, Canada, and the United Kingdom.

The contact information given to me by Sue and Randy Rice allowed me to reach out to several other people involved with Korean human rights, and I began writing them letters after I arrived in the United States. One of these activists was Pharis Harvey, the executive director of the North American Coalition for Human Rights in Korea, which focused on lobbying in Washington. Pharis had spent time in Japan in the 1970s while involved with the United Methodist Church and had played a role in getting information out of Korea. In fact, some of the material I had mailed or directly brought out of Korea had made its way to him. He had been told I was returning to the United States, so when we talked, he wanted to learn what I had seen in Kwangju and how the dissidents were reacting to the dictatorship. I told him what I knew about how the protests in Seoul and Kwangju in May 1980 were organized, how the common people felt about the dictatorship, and how the information pipeline operated. I only met with him in Washington twice, but we kept in touch by mail, and occasionally by phone, and he provided me with updates about the information he was getting out of Korea.

Because I shared my contact information with anyone interested, I was also contacted by Choi Sung-il, director of the Council for Democracy in Korea. He wanted a witness to provide firsthand testimony about 5.18 to those in the Korean community, so in early 1982 he asked me to speak about what I experienced in Kwangju at a Korean church in Washington, D.C. I wrote the speech in Korean and then asked a Korean classmate if he could read through it and correct my errors. This classmate had just started in my program and was the son of a well-known tuberculosis researcher at Yonsei University who I had met when I was in the Peace Corps. Within a month of him reading my speech, his father had him transferred to another university because he did not want his son associating with a radical.

In Washington I met with Choi Sung-il and was taken to the church where I would give the talk. The congregation was made up of Korean-

Americans who were active in the movement for democracy and human rights in Korea. When I gave the speech, I was only able to make it part of the way through before I was overcome with emotion. I was unable to fight back tears, so one of the other speakers took over and finished my speech for me.

That same year I was asked to speak about Kwangju at the National Press Club in Washington, D.C. I met Pharis Harvey there and was also introduced to Lee Shin-bom. Lee had been a law student at Seoul National University when he was arrested in June 1980 and was sentenced to nine years in prison. He was released after two years due to pressure from Amnesty International, and after that, as a condition of his release, he went to the United States to live in exile. I found him to be very humble and he didn't like to talk about what he had experienced. He sometimes spoke of going back to Korea, even though he would be immediately arrested if he did. For the Press Club talk, Lee did the calligraphy for a poster that was displayed with "Kwangju" written in Hangeul over red splatters. He told me his tradition-minded father would have approved of the poster's message but would have disapproved of the calligraphy because it did not use Chinese characters.

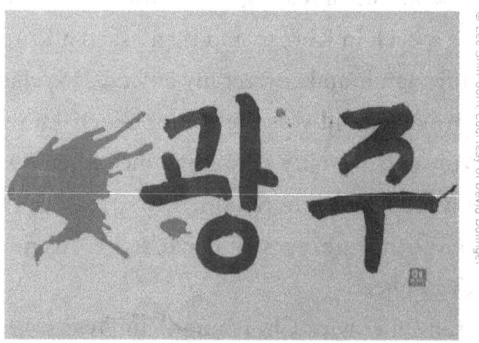

Lee Shin-bom's calligraphy

At this time, I was kept informed of the Korea-related activities of the Presbyterian missionary community through contacts provided by the Rices and my grandmother. My elderly grandmother was a leader in her Presbyterian church, and she and my mother had been active in the campaign to save Kim Dae-jung. Whenever I needed to talk to people in the Presbyterian church, my grandmother made the necessary introductions and put me in contact with the right people.

In late 1984, I was contacted by Ed Baker, who worked at the Harvard-Yenching Institute. A former PCV, he had been politically active in Korea in the late 1960s and 1970s, had worked with Choi Sung-il on the campaign to save Kim Dae-jung's life in 1980, and had helped bring Kim Dae-jung to Harvard in 1983. He asked if I would like to participate in the International Commission on Kwangju, and I attended its first meeting at a restaurant in New York City in January 1985. Other members of the commission who I had previous connections to included Choi Sung-il, Lee Shin-bom, Faye Moon's husband Stephen, and Carolyn, my fellow K-45 PCV who had smuggled my photos out of Korea. There were six former PCVs on the executive committee, including Linda Lewis, who as a graduate student had also witnessed the Kwangju Uprising, and Professors David McCann and Bruce Cumings.

The commission was focused on sharing stories of repression in Korea and communicating the truth of what had happened in Kwangju, and to that end we did such things as taking out a full-page ad in *The New York Times*, identifying additional potential witnesses, and getting information out concerning the Samcheong re-education camps, where thousands of "socially unfit" people and critics of Chun's regime were "purified" through hard labor. All of this was organized over the phone or by writing letters. Considering how easy it is to communicate and organize today, it is amazing what we were able to accomplish at that time. It took lots of effort to stay in contact with people, but luckily my experience in Korea of writing letters to my parents every week helped prepare me for this.

The commission also played a role in organizing the protests against Chun Doo-hwan's visit to Washington in April 1985. Despite being busy with graduate school, I met with the organizers prior to the protests to help provide suggestions. When we had lunch at a Korean restaurant not far from the Pentagon, I was told as we walked in that I shouldn't talk about Kwangju or the protests. This was because the restaurant was frequented by Koreans associated with the Korean government, as well as by people who were spying on Koreans living in the United States. When Chun arrived in Washington he was greeted by billboards, posters, and protesters wearing T-shirts with the red-splatter "Kwangju" logo Lee Shin-bom had designed.

During these years when I was engrossed in graduate school and Korean human rights work, I didn't have many chances to talk to Tim. I tried writing him when he was in Korea, but I assumed that the letters never reached him since I got no letters from him. Before I left Korea, we had talked about the fact that we would probably not be able to stay in touch because of what we had been through. I knew he was trying to keep a low profile to protect his Korean friends. In 1986 he returned to the United States to attend graduate school at the University of Hawaii. We talked on the phone a few times after his return, though not as often as I wished we had.

During one of our phone calls Tim told me that he was writing a paper about the Kwangju Uprising, for which he wanted to use our firsthand accounts. I was surprised when he told me that this would be the first academic journal article to be published about the Kwangju Uprising. I agreed to share what I had written for the UNCHR petition and other talks that I had given. Tim's article, "The Kwangju Uprising: An Inside View," was published in the journal *Korean Studies* in 1987, and, because it is based on eyewitness accounts, it is still relevant 30 years later.

© Hankokilbo

Citizens taking part in pro-democracy demonstrations, June 1987.

In June 1987 I paid close attention to the events unfolding in Korea, where not only students but also the middle class took part in protests demanding direct presidential elections. That the protests included people other than students reminded me of Kwangju. I was happy to see this happen and to see the protesters' success, but I was also sad that it took so long after 5.18 to finally occur. Though university students acted as the conscience of the country, once they graduated, they became more worried about their day-to-day existence than the future of the entire country. This wasn't surprising. We had all heard stories of people losing their jobs and being blacklisted for union work or for voicing their opinions regarding democracy, and these people, the burgeoning middle-class, had too much to lose. But the events of 1987, particularly the deaths of two students, caused them to stand up and say enough was enough.

The images of the protests and student Lee Han-yeol's death caused by a tear gas cannister brought to mind what happened in Kwangju in May

1980, but instead of two deaths, Kwangju had so many more, and the entire city had been brutalized. Though I was happy to see people finally stand up, I was sad that it had taken seven more years than it should have. It was also depressing to see that the opposition could not come together in unity, and that their egos led to Roh Tae-woo, Chun Doo-hwan's right-hand man, being elected president. Many U.S.-based Korea observers worried that the end of the dictatorship had all been orchestrated and that after the 1988 Summer Olympics in Seoul the government would revert to authoritarian rule. Even in the early 1990s I was still very concerned about the potential for Korea to backslide and lose the gains it had made, and it wasn't until Kim Young-sam's election that I finally felt I could relax a little.

In 1990 I was contacted by a woman I had met through the Philadelphia-based Korean Human Rights group. She was helping to organize an event at Harvard University commemorating the tenth anniversary of the Kwangju Uprising titled "In Memory of Kwangju: Our Blood, Our Tears." It was sponsored by the Korean Thursday Prayer Group in New England, a group of Korean students from Boston-area universities. I was asked if I wanted to participate, and as a result I attended the event and spoke about what I saw and did during 5.18, while other participants contributed to the memorial in various ways, such as by performing plays and singing songs.

While I was in Boston, I slept on the floor of one of the organizers. This was because, after defending my thesis and receiving my Ph.D. in December 1987, I had begun a post-doctoral position at Princeton, but it did not pay much. I usually had very little money left at the end of each month. When I was finishing my Ph.D., my adviser tried to convince me to stay in academia because he believed that the private sector was where the not-so-bright Ph.D. went. I explained that I wanted to be in the diagnostics industry because I felt I could have a greater impact on

David speaking at Harvard, on the tenth anniversary of the Kwangju Uprising, while wearing a t-shirt with Lee Shin-bom's 'Kwangju' calligraphy on it.

peoples' lives by using my skills to develop knowledge and tests that could correctly diagnose their illnesses. Being able to accurately identify a disease affecting an individual is essential to providing effective treatment. Despite these goals, doing a post-doc was considered a part of the Ph.D. process. My position was in a lab where I learned microbial genetics and was able to develop my skills. I spent two years at Princeton, but while I learned a great deal there, I also discovered that the politics in academia were ridiculous and I wanted nothing to do with them. In 1990, I made my move from academia to the private sector.

The previous year, I had taken another step in my life when I married Anne, whom I had met at graduate school in 1982, where she was studying biochemistry. We carried on a long-distance relationship after she left Temple in 1984 to get her Ph.D. in cell biology from the University of New York, Stony Brook, on Long Island. We finally married in 1989 at her parish church in Philadelphia, with her uncle presiding. In September 1992, our son Tim, who was named in part after Tim Warnberg, was born. His early arrival by more than a week left me rushing to get from Vermont, where I had gone after a conference to take part in a bike race, to Princeton, where Anne was doing a post-doctoral fellowship.

By that point I had started working at Schering Plough, a pharmaceutical company, where I focused on the development of tests to help screen compounds for new drug entities. Unfortunately, I didn't feel that this research was focused on anything other than contributing to the well-being of those living in high-income countries. Disappointed with this, I went to Colorado to work for a start-up, but despite the fact I was using technology to try and develop better diagnostics, it was still focused on diseases specific to high-income countries. At that point in my life, I had fallen into the same trap that had confined Koreans after they graduated from university, in which I was too focused on my day-to-day existence, but I didn't realize it at the time.

While attending a conference in Washington, D.C. in 1994, I contacted a former K-45 PCV and happened to ask him if he knew how Tim was doing. Tim had called my parents' house a few years earlier, after I had moved to Princeton, but he hadn't left a phone number, so I wasn't able to contact him. In answer to my question, I found out that Tim had died from the complications of HIV. I was saddened to hear this news and realize I wouldn't get to spend more time with him. Tim was a good person, someone I'm proud to say I knew and had the chance to learn from. His death reminded me that we don't appreciate the time we have with people because we always assume there will be more. Ultimately, learning of Tim's death made me stop and re-evaluate my approach to life. I realized I was taking too much for granted and that I needed to take control of where I was going. In that way, Tim put me back on track. He also made me want to focus on HIV diagnostics.

In 1996 an opportunity presented itself to work for a start-up in Jackson Hole, Wyoming, that was strictly focused on HIV and was supporting clinical trials for new antiretroviral drugs to help HIV-infected individuals. I jumped at this chance. After some time, I moved to a company where I was part of a team that developed a test that helped to ensure that HIV-positive individuals were receiving effective therapies. It monitored mutations that caused resistance to the antiretroviral drugs being used to treat individuals with HIV. The test was too late to help Tim, but it has helped millions of others around the world.

After that, I made many more career moves in which I focused on shifting the diagnostics paradigm from confirmation of a clinician's best guess to true diagnostics that provide actionable information that can be used by general healthcare providers to provide better and informed care management. Throughout my career, I also stayed focused and up to date on tuberculosis diagnostics and treatment, and always tried to convince the companies I worked for to develop tests specifically for TB. I usually had no luck because the companies did not understand the disease, or the potential impact proper diagnostics could have. Fortunately, from 2013 to 2017 I worked for an NGO in Geneva that was strictly focused on diagnostics and those marginalized in healthcare systems in low- and-middle-income countries. It was there that I was able to influence a change in approach to diagnosing and treating those with TB. My goal has always been to develop tests that would lead to better care management for individuals. I have prioritized the people being treated during the development of a test to create tests that can have a better impact on an individual's well-being.

Return to Korea

It was through my work that I was able to return to Korea in 2005 for the first time in 24 years. I was working for Bayer Diagnostics and needed to make a work-related trip to Japan, so I convinced my boss that I should also visit the Bayer office in Korea. This trip allowed me to go down to Kwangju for a day and visit the May 18th National Cemetery and the May 18 Memorial Foundation. A year later, in 2006, I returned to Korea for a two-week visit with my family and toured the country. I got to spend time in Kwangju and Yeongam, and during that trip I was shown a pamphlet with a picture of Tim carrying a stretcher and was asked if it was me. I explained that it was Tim Warnberg, a fellow Peace Corps Volunteer who had since passed away. A few years later I was contacted by the Korean broadcaster SBS and asked to take part in a documentary they were making for the 30th anniversary of the Kwangju Uprising. A reporter and a cameraman came to Boston and stayed at our house while filming an interview with me, and then in early May 2010 I went to Korea and was filmed in Yeongam and Kwangju.

For one of the interviews, SBS brought me to the Provincial Capital to speak with some of the student leaders I had met there in 1980. There I met with Kim Tae-jong, a student leader I remembered seeing in the Provincial Capital and speaking from the fountain during a rally, Jeon Yong-ho, co-author of the banned 1985 book *Kwangju Diary*, and Kim Yun-gi. It was exciting to see them again after so much time had passed. Because I had no names, only faces to remember, I had not known whether they had survived, with one exception.

After the four of us talked for some time, Kim Yun-gi asked me if we had met in the street after 5.18. I said yes. In fact, when I first saw him that day, I realized he was the person I had crossed paths with in Kwangju when I went back to Yeongam to pack up my things, but I was astonished that he remembered me as well. When we met that day in June 1980, we'd had no choice but to avoid openly acknowledging each other. I didn't probe too deeply about his experience that day, however. He was

Meeting again after 30 years, in May of 2010. From left to right, Kim Tae-jong, Kim Yun-gi. David Dolinger, and Jeon Yong-ho.

the quietest of the three, and I wondered if, like me, he had still not fully come to grips with what had happened 30 years ago. I guessed that he still had the same pain I do when it comes to 5.18. It is a pain and a sorrow that cannot be suppressed and makes remembering and talking about the events of that time very difficult. All I can do is stumble as I speak, try to suppress the tears, and hope that I can change the subject. Even in the writing of this memoir I have had to fight back tears as I recalled memories of 5.18 and its aftermath. I try to focus on my time in Korea before 5.18 and put aside my memories of what happened in Kwangju, but they are always there just below the surface.

When the plans were made with SBS for me to return to Kwangju to do the final set of interviews, I decided to ask the Korean government about attending the ceremony commemorating the 30th anniversary of the Kwangju Uprising. I was lucky enough to be introduced to a very resourceful woman who helped secure my invitation, and who also put me in contact with the May 18 Memorial Foundation. The foundation arranged for me to speak at a press conference while I was in Kwangju and invited me to the opening of the Gwangju Asia Forum. On May 18, 2010, I attended the 30th anniversary ceremony at the May 18th National Cemetery. It was impressive to see that after 30 years people were able to come together to remember what happened in May 1980. But it was sad to see that so many lacked closure. How does one deal with the sudden loss of a child, a father, a wife, and of the future they embodied? How do mothers who are still dealing with their loss do so in a place which is a tribute to the historical moment during which their child died? I couldn't help but worry that it was being turned into a political event, when it should be a time of remembrance and a time for those of us who remain to comfort those dealing with the void left behind by the loss of a loved one.

During an evening get-together I was again asked about the photo of Tim carrying a stretcher and learned that the May 18 Memorial Foundation had still not identified him. I told them Tim's story, wrote his name down for them, and later, after I returned home, provided them with additional information.

At the press conference arranged by the May 18 Memorial Foundation during my visit, I spoke with several reporters who asked me questions about my involvement in the Kwangju Uprising. During this interview I let it be known that because the May 18th National Cemetery was open for all participants in the uprising, I wanted to have part of my ashes interred at the cemetery. I then learned that a year earlier the German reporter Jürgen Hinzpeter had asked to be interred there as well. The city of Gwangju later decided to deny both of our requests, but stated that we could be buried in Mangwol-dong Cemetery and told me that a small amount of my ashes or nail clippings could be placed in the May 18th

National Cemetery. I would also like a part of me to be placed at the top of Wolchulsan by my son. Wolchulsan was a place where I spent a lot of time reflecting on who I was and who I could become. To me it is a special, spiritual place, and I would like to become a part of the circle of life there.

17. Closing Thoughts

What follows is a summary of my "truths" concerning my experiences in Korea during and after the Kwangju Uprising. I know I may be told that some of my conclusions are incorrect, that I did not know the whole story, or that my Korean was not good enough to understand the subtleties of what I was being told, but in this book, I have presented these truths based upon what I saw, felt, and learned from my conversations with people. My truths are:

- Citizens were brutally murdered during 5.18. In normal circumstances, the perpetrators, including all of the high ranking officers, should have stood trial for these crimes and should have apologized to the citizens of Kwangju.
- Citizens were shot at from helicopters and were injured or killed as a result.

- Citizens were shot with bullets that fragmented and were designed to cause as much internal damage as possible. These bullets are outlawed for use against soldiers of another nation during wartime, but not against one's own citizens.[14]
- Citizens took up arms for what they believed was a justifiable reason: to protect their lives, their friends and family's lives, and the city.
- After the martial law troops were pushed out on May 21, Kwangju did not fall into disarray. Citizens did not riot and loot.
- Citizens cleaned the streets, organized the defense of the city, and looked out for one another.
- Citizens returned to the Provincial Capital the arms that had been seized.
- Citizens wanted a peaceful outcome.
- Citizens hoped the U.S. government would intervene to bring about a peaceful outcome.
- As early as May 21, foreign journalists were asked to contact the U.S. Embassy, but for days replied only that reporters should never become a part of the news.
- Citizens died for what they believed in and for the future of their children, the future of the unborn, and the future of Korea.
- This book's focus on the actions of men during the Kwangju Uprising is mainly due to the fact that I mostly interacted with men. I do not want to underplay the role of women during 5.18 or within

---

[14] The 1899 Hague Declaration concerning expanding bullets prohibits the use, as a means of warfare, of "bullets which expand or flatten easily in the human body." Pursuant to Article 8(2)(b)(xix) of the 1998 Rome Statute of the International Criminal Court, "[e]mploying bullets which expand or flatten easily in the human body" constitutes a war crime in international armed conflicts.

the democracy movement in Korea. From my narrative, it may seem as if women did not play an important role during the Kwangju Uprising which is not true at all. Women were the backbone of both the democracy movement and during those days in May of 1980. During the Kwangju Uprising, women were brutalized by troops representing the Korean government, physically, mentally and sexually, and they were beaten, bayoneted and shot to death, but despite being aware of these potential outcomes they still took part and were willing to sacrifice for others and the future of Korea. During the Kwangju Uprising, they were the sisters, mothers and grandmothers who provided the strength that reinforced the men. I should have talked with them more, but it was painful to do so, especially when the interaction was at the level of a sister, mother, or grandmother. After Kwangju, it was women who took me under their wings and introduced me to the inner workings of the democracy movement. Women are the main strength of Korea and I apologize for not talking with them more during May of 1980.

These are my truths and I stand by them.

On the topic of Kwangju's citizens arming themselves to stand up to the military, the "Why we took up arms" statement declared that "to protect this place and to protect our parents, brothers and sisters, we each held guns in our hands." This reminded me of the elderly gentleman Tim, and I met on the evening of May 18, who had stated, "We can't let them treat us like this!" It also reminded me of the "Declaration of the Causes and Necessity of Taking Up Arms," which was adopted by the Second Congressional Congress of the United States on July 6, 1775, to justify the beginning of the American Revolution, and which stated that as "a people attacked by unprovoked enemies... in defense of the freedom that is our birth-right... we have taken up arms."

Despite these similarities, my own experiences in May 1980 and the subsequent release of declassified diplomatic cables have made it clear to me that the U.S. government was far more involved in decisions related to the suppression of the Kwangju Uprising than it has been willing to admit. On more than one occasion during visits to Korea I have had U.S. Embassy staff or other Americans confront me and tell me that my opinions in this regard are wrong, are doing a disservice to the United States, and could hurt the relationship between the United States and the Republic of Korea.

My response to such criticism has been to state that the best path forward for the United States would be to apologize for its actions—or lack thereof—during the Kwangju Uprising and to ask the people of Kwangju, the families of those lost, and the people of Korea for forgiveness. Even if the conclusions I have drawn from the declassified documents and my personal experiences are wrong, the U.S. government should still apologize because, whether directly or indirectly, we played a role in what occurred and the subsequent outcome.

I am proud of the citizens of Kwangju. I do not regret what I did. I was honored to be told that I was a citizen of Kwangju by citizen leaders in the Provincial Capital. I have always made it a point whenever I am in Korea to visit the May 18th National Cemetery, and I have been lucky enough to attend the memorial service there on several occasions. In 2013, when the mothers of the victims marched up the aisle and sang the prohibited song "March for the Beloved," which led to President Park Geun-hye leaving the ceremony early, I stood in support of them, singing as best I could.

A part of me died in Kwangju, but another part of me was born or awakened because of what I witnessed in May 1980. I regret that I did not do more to help the citizens of Kwangju during 5.18 and that will be a regret that I will live with until my dying days. I send my deepest apologies to the citizens of Kwangju and to the fallen for not having done more.

Part IV

Remembering Tim

The iconic photo of the previously-unknown foreigner, Tim Warnberg, carrying a wounded citizen to Chonnam University Hospital on May 19, 1980.

Tim Warnberg was born on November 3, 1954 to Charles Warnberg and Lorraine Koop Warnberg. He was the third of eight children and grew up in Brainerd, a small city of 12,000 people in central Minnesota. He attended the University of Minnesota, Morris, joined the Peace Corps and went to Korea in 1978, and took Korean classes at Yonsei University from 1981. He began graduate studies at the University of Hawaii in 1986, but died on February 7, 1993 before he could receive his Ph.D.

While attending the University of Hawaii, Tim Warnberg researched and wrote the article "The Kwangju Uprising: An Inside View," which was published in Volume 11 of the academic journal *Korean Studies* in 1987. This article is therefore the first academic article to be published about 5.18, and it is reprinted in full in Chapter 20 of this book.

Despite being 35 years old, "The Kwangju Uprising: An Inside View" is still relevant to anyone with an interest in the events that occurred in Kwangju in May 1980. This is due in particular to the fact that Tim drew upon the eyewitness accounts written by himself, his fellow Peace Corps Volunteers, and the missionaries in Kwangju, in addition to supplementing these with archival research.

This well-researched and well-written article will also help to give readers a sense of Tim Warnberg's scholarly abilities, and a deeper appreciation for what he might have further contributed to the study of Korea.

18. Memories of Tim

by His Family

Wanting Tim to be better remembered, what follows is a collection of memories gathered from people who knew Tim, beginning with a conversation with his eldest sister, Roxanne Wilson, and lifelong friend, Keevie Fairbanks, who reflected upon his life in an online video chat on August 15, 2021.

Roxanne Wilson:

Tim had a tremendous curiosity and nurtured friendships with people from many different backgrounds. My dad had this same curiosity. He was the longest-serving sheriff in Crow Wing County and treated both prisoners and influential people with respect and compassion. He would often tell us there was a fine line between those who were in jail and those who were not; the line was often poverty. He genuinely liked people and could talk easily to anyone. He had a remarkable ability to connect with people through stories and humor. He was bright, funny, and witty. He

The Warnberg family. Tim, at far right in the back row, stands next to his parents, Lorraine and Charles.

wasn't a typical sheriff.

Both of my parents were very liberal for their era. My mom stayed at home and was quieter. She was devoted to caring for others through her cooking and baking. She created a home that was warm and inviting to neighbors, friends, and persons in need. She would bake bread and make meals for people who had just had a baby, were sick, sad, or lonely. My dad would deliver the meals and brighten their day with a story and a joke. My parents wanted the recipients to feel visible, important and loved. My mom also invited into our home people who might be struggling. My siblings and I remember getting up in the morning to be greeted by a woman who had spent a significant amount of time at the state hospital sitting at the kitchen table, smoking, and having coffee while my mom served her breakfast. We didn't always like this as kids, but we witnessed our parents' lives as "givers."

Our family holiday stories are full of stories of colorful people who were "down on their luck" or vulnerable joining us to celebrate. My mom was influenced by her mother who was widowed at a young age with five children. She was very poor and not connected to her husband's wealthy family in Brainerd who would not help her because she was Lutheran, not Catholic. Despite her poverty, my grandma would make sandwiches to serve to hobos

Charles and Lorraine Warnberg in the 1950s.

who rode the trains and knew her house was a safe haven. We grew up very close to the aunts, uncles, and cousins and developed such as bond in growing up. We went to the "Lake" every year as a large family and Tim kept those relationships through his life.

Tim had my dad's ability to connect with others and my mom, aunts, and grandma's skills of extending hospitality.

Keevie Fairbanks:

Tim was the best of both of his parents. And just to elaborate on that story, my sister was a single parent when she had her child, and Lorraine, Tim's mother, sent a complete dinner and had her husband deliver it. I recently found out at class reunions that such things, including preparing and sharing food, and inviting over people who were challenged or vulnerable during the holidays, were very common with the Warnbergs. They impacted many of my classmates. There were always a variety of people at his house, so I think that's where Tim picked it up and went forward in his life.

Roxanne Wilson:

Tim was academically high achieving, popular, and gifted athletically. He won all sorts of track and field awards. I think he set records in high hurdles in Brainerd that took years to beat. He was very well liked as a child, but probably more so as a teenager. He was six feet tall and blond and had long hair all through high school and college. He really was nice looking, connected easily with

Tim Warnberg with long hair, before he moved to Korea.

people, was confident, but not arrogant. At the same time, he was aware he was gay, but kept that hidden.

Keevie Fairbanks:

Tim stood out—he really did—and he liked unique people and I guess that's the category I'm in. I met him when I was transitioning from a Catholic School and I didn't know many public-school kids. He approached me on the step of his neighbor's house and asked, "You attend the Catholic School, right?" From that point we started talking, but what really connected us was music. We both liked music that wasn't the usual type of music our classmates liked. They liked heavy rock, but we liked Janis Joplin. Janis was a really wild soul, especially for people like us who came from a small town. Her music became the basis for a lifelong friendship.

Roxanne Wilson:

He did love music—music was a way for him to come together with people.

Keevie Fairbanks:

And he could talk to anyone—he was fearless. Even if there was someone who was begging for change, he would take the time to speak to them. He was fearless in other ways. I've hitchhiked with Tim, and even jumped a train with him. Janis Joplin was going to be in playing in Canada, so we figured out what savings we had and jumped on a train, not realizing the train stopped at the Brainerd paper mill. The next thing we heard was a voice saying, "Get out, you guys." Since Tim's dad was the county sheriff, we got off!

He was also really well-read and was constantly reading. As far back as I can remember, when I went over to his house, he would be on the front porch reading anything he could get his hands on. His curiosity was unmatched. And he stood up for people—he stood up for me. That's the type of person he was.

Roxanne Wilson:

There were two sisters in our school who were obese, obviously poor, and terribly bullied by the other students. Years after Tim was gone from Brainerd, I was talking to one of the sisters and she asked me about Tim and said, "You know, Tim was my only friend in high school." As she put it, "He was so popular, but he came to my house and he would visit with us and we would talk about what was going on in our lives," and, she added, "I always felt like he liked me, and he treated me like I was important." It just struck me at the time that this was classically Tim. He would engage with someone who was in the corners of life who he felt was important and interesting. I don't think he did it just to be nice—

that really wasn't his style. I think he really did want to hear her story and about her life. What was striking to me was that, even years later, she talked about how much it meant to her that he saw her as a person.

Keevie Fairbanks:

Tim was a pivotal part of my adolescence. He nominated my name for student body president when we were seniors, and I won—with his help of course. He was always pushing himself and others, and that in itself was truly a gift he gave to me. I was very fortunate to be one of his closest friends. And I will forever be grateful, not only to Tim, but to the Warnbergs—they really were my second family.

Roxanne Wilson:

Tim spent one or two summers hitchhiking around the country. He was a really good writer, and in some of his journals he wrote pages and pages describing who he rode with, what they said, and what he thought of them. They are less about how he was feeling and more about developing the story of what the actual hitchhiking experience and relationships were like.

He also spent summers working as a camp counselor for kids with diabetes. After he graduated from high school, he went to the University of Minnesota-Morris. I think he originally went there on a track scholarship with the intent to go into medical school.

During his college years he spent a summer doing a bike ride from Toronto to Miami with three friends, which was sponsored by Sekine bicycle company. They biked, camped, or stayed with people they met along the way. This was very typical of him in that he liked to meet new people and let the experience shape him. He was always a little more daring and more willing to forge ahead into new territory. Years later, when Keevie and I would join him on outings to riskier places, we were a bit more cautious, and he would accuse us of letting our fears influence our ability to experience something new.

When he graduated from the University of Minnesota, he took the MCAT to go to medical school. He didn't do well enough and decided to go into the Peace Corp to improve his chances for medical school admission. His placement in Korea provided him with one of the great joys of his life. He loved the language, culture, and friends he made. His work with people who were diagnosed with Hansen's disease was meaningful. I think the whole experience transformed his perception of the world.

David Dolinger:

I think the work he was doing helped him learn more about human nature and the need to be there for people. It is important to remember that we, as Peace Corps Volunteers, were on the front line of finding individuals infected with Hansen's disease or tuberculosis. One Saturday night in Kwangju, something was clearly on Tim's mind, and eventually he told me what was bothering him. The day before he'd had to tell an individual that he had Hansen's disease. At this time in Korea this was one of the worst things that you could find out. You were ostracized by friends, family, and society, and would end up having to live in a special village. What bothered him most was that as he had been talking with the young man, he had discovered that the man was just weeks away from getting married. The diagnosis put an end to that, and Tim felt both that it was unfair but also that he bore some responsibility for the end of the marriage plans. We talked about how hard it was to be the person responsible for sharing news that sometimes drastically changed a person's life, how we had to be careful in the way we told people, and how we might be able to convey the news in a hopeful manner. Looking back on it now, I wish that I could have said something

Tim Warnberg and David Dolinger at a Hansen's Disease village near Kwangju.

more to help him feel better.

On a more upbeat note, when the PCVs working in the health centers in South Jeolla Province went to Kwangju on the weekends to hang out, the first person we looked for was Tim. That was his city, he knew all the places to go, and we were always meeting people who knew him. "We're all invited to dinner with a bunch of doctors? Oh, wow, this should be fun." You never knew what the adventure was going to be, but as long as you were willing to go along with it, it was always fun. He had great stories, like how he hitchhiked to San Francisco. I was rather naïve, and could only think, "Wow, who is this guy? He goes out and does whatever he wants!"

With Tim as well, if you were stranded in Kwangju, you knew where he lived, and it was no problem to drop in. You would always have a place to stay for the night. Tim and I also spent a lot of time in music bars in Kwangju. I loved to go and listen to music, and he knew the best places, as well as which ones had live bands rather than DJs. His knowledge of these places went beyond Kwangju. Once, when we were in Seoul, he introduced me to a club in Itaewon, a place I almost never went, but it had Bose 901 speakers placed around the room and had a great LP selection. He also told me about a jazz club he had found when he had traveled in Japan, in Osaka I think, which had a wall of 901s.

Keevie Fairbanks:

That was one of the gifts that Tim had, knowing all the places to go. It was because he took the time to talk to people, to ask strangers what was going on and discover these things due to his curious nature.

Roxanne Wilson:

Tim wrote a letter in early 1980 in which he related what it was like being in Korea and how difficult it was, especially initially, because he was a white, blond-haired person. He described how behavior that was outrageous for Korean people was even more outrageous if a white person did it, so he felt like he was always onstage representing America, whether he wanted to or not.

He wrote about what it was like to experience that sort of isolation, where he was always so aware of who he was and what he looked like, and how he had come to value those close relationships where he could be true to himself around the people he was with. At the time, he was trying to decide if he was going to leave Korea. In some ways, to be "offstage" would be helpful, but in other ways the intensity of those "behind-the-scenes" friendships was such a valuable experience that it would be like being ripped away from something vital. As it turned out, these friendships would last throughout his entire life.

My parents called me when Kwangju was in the news. My dad was watching the news for any word about Tim. At the time, we had no idea about the actions Tim had taken. We were simply frightened he might have been hurt. My dad called me when he heard from Tim after a week of worrying. He told my dad he was fine, which was a huge relief. We heard the details and saw pictures later when he came home to visit. It was obvious he was profoundly saddened and angered by what he witnessed. He felt both the Korean government and the American military could have handled Kwangju without such violence. He said the American military should have come forward with their influence to stop what was happening. He would later say his role in what happened in Kwangju made it difficult for him to return to Korea, as the government would not let him in. I don't know all the details but remember that statement.

Charles Warnberg:

On May 30, 1980, Tim Warnberg's hometown paper, the Brainerd Dispatch, published an article written by Tim Sloan titled "Tim Warnberg survives Korean riots." It reported that a week of worry and sleepless nights had ended for Crow Wing County sheriff Charles Warnberg when he got a phone call from his son, who had arrived in Seoul.

"He called me at 7 this morning," a relieved [Charles] Warnberg said today. "It was kind of hard to even hear him, and he couldn't talk for long." [...]

"We hadn't heard from him since the thing began," Warnberg said. "All the phone lines were down." [...]

"I was watching television one night and I could see machine guns on the top of the roof at the hospital where he worked," Warnberg said. [...]

"He was right in the thick of it," Warnberg said of his son. "He said he saw some of his friends beaten to death with clubs, right in front of him."

Knowing that Tim was ordered to leave Kwangju but did not, the newspaper wondered if Charles Warnberg had given his son "a little fatherly criticism" for refusing to leave.

"He probably wouldn't have listened to me anyway," Warnberg laughed. "He's pretty independent. And compassionate."

Keevie Fairbanks:

Tim came out to me in 1980 or 1981 when he was home from Korea for a visit, and came to see me in Minneapolis. I had come out myself two or three years earlier and was angry at the fact that he had waited so long to tell me. I told him, "Tell Roxanne—she needs to know." But it wasn't an easy thing to do. Before the law changed in 1973, we could have been put in the state mental hospital, so there was a lot of fear, especially coming from a small town. As well, let's not forget the impact of Christianity. It was a combination of fear, guilt, and shame.

Roxanne Wilson:

He certainly talked about not feeling safe as a gay person. He told me of some of his early experiences with a Christian minister. When he was in the seventh or eighth grade, in a confirmation class, I think he had an experience that profoundly affected him. Somebody asked about homosexuals and the minister who was teaching the class told them, "That's absolutely disgusting. They're disgusting people." He talked about thinking, "That is me." Perhaps that led to him developing a sense of shame that delayed him coming out to his family and friends.

Tim came out to me in a letter in 1981, but he didn't tell the rest of my family until he was forced to because he had AIDS. He was a closeted gay individual in his early years, and I think one reason he wanted to hear and learn about people's stories was that he realized he had his own hidden story. He talked about knowing he was "different" at a very early age. He wanted to leave Brainerd and get out and be part of the larger world. In the places he went beyond Brainerd he began discovering gay communities and friends. He knew what it felt like to be marginalized and to have an identity that was highly regarded and popular. He struggled over how to present himself to the world.

He moved to Hawaii in 1985 to get a Ph.D. in Korean literature from the University of Hawaii. He studied under Marshall Pihl, and for his dissertation he translated into English a book of *sijo* poetry by Jo Jong-hyeon[15] titled *Jajeong ui Jigu* (Earth at Midnight). He was very happy in Hawaii because he was immersed in Korean language and poetry, was living in an academic world, was out as gay person, and was enjoying the beauty of the island. By 1991 his dissertation was almost complete. Tim's dream was to finish translating several poems from the book, finish his dissertation, and get hired at the Institute of East Asian Studies at Berkeley.

When Tim became seriously ill due to AIDS, he decided to return to Brainerd. He called us in November or December of 1991 and told us that he was dying, and when he came home for Christmas, he was so skeletal I thought he would die. He went back to Hawaii, and when I flew out there and saw him in the hospital, I was shocked at the poor quality of the care he was receiving. I didn't realize how bad it was in Hawaii at the time. We flew back home, and I was able to get him health care in Minnesota and took him to a doctor in Minneapolis. Though Tim was skeletally ill, the

---

[15] Jo Jong-hyeon (1906-1989), born in Goheung, South Jeolla Province, was a Buddhist monk, independence activist, teacher, and poet. His poetry focused on Buddhist themes and nature, and Earth at Midnight, his first poetry collection, was published in 1969. Jo is the father of well-known author Jo Jeong-rae. Tim's copy of Earth at Midnight was signed by Jo Jong-hyeon on June 20, 1988.

doctor started him on new meds which really revived him. He gained a lot of weight and began to look very healthy, and once his strength returned, he traveled back to Hawaii quite frequently to visit friends and went to San Francisco as well. He was on Ganciclovir and had IVs, and since I'm a nurse I went with him to Hawaii and California two or three times and administered his medication. He spent travel time with Jin, his partner, Noren and Lee, Conrad, Su and Keyes, Keola and Martin...all people who valued him and made him feel loved.

Coming home was challenging for him. He talked about what a shock it was to go from one world to another. My parents and family did not hesitate to welcome him home and to create a haven of love and healing. We decided with Tim in the very beginning to share with others that he had AIDS. Tim, my parents, the teenage grandchildren, and his family all spoke openly of his illness. This was a deliberate decision to come out of the shadow of stigma, to show our love for each other and to break the stigma for others. In each of the worlds he had lived, he'd had friendships and families and people that he connected to with whom he felt safe. In Brainerd he was cared for but felt the judgment of Christianity again. This was particularly painful when one of his friends wrote him a long letter saying that unless he repented, he would go to hell. When he dealt with these righteous Christians, he was angry, but on the other hand he was still kind in the way he approached them—unlike my other brothers who were more furious with them. He wrote his friend a long, thoughtful letter in return to try to open his mind. Tim also went to schools and talked about HIV or talked about Korea and what a wonderful country it was. He got somewhat involved with the Rural AIDS Action Network. He also connected with the gay community in St. Cloud, which was larger than Brainerd, and attended dinners and parties. He influenced in various ways the older grandkids in our family who still remember him, particularly in being more open to people who are gay, speaking up thoughtfully for others, and traveling all over the world.

He was very adamant that he was going to live until he died. Though I was busy raising two kids who were 11 and 13 at the time, I went up to Brainerd three or four times a week. He wanted to go to concerts, so we went to see Bruce Springsteen. We went to Korean restaurants and plays in Minneapolis, visited Keevie, and travelled back to Hawaii. We went to California to see his dear friends Su and Keyes. He refused to have his whole world be the illness. My sister lived in Brainerd and saw him daily. My other brothers and sister and their families visited often, as did Tim's friends, cousins, aunts, and uncles from all over the world. He created a sense of coming together during this final journey and all those who loved him stepped into the circle to hold each other in love and in pain. The group who surrounded him included family, people he knew from Korea, friends from Hawaii and California, Peace Corps volunteers, friends, college friends and his partner Jin. Much of this happened in the same kitchen and family room he grew up in and would eventually die in. As my parents watched their young son die, they also welcomed all these people in for coffee, bread, and time with Tim.

After Tim's health recovered due to the treatment he received in Minnesota, he travelled and met friends and kept busy for about a year before he became very sick again in late 1992. He was 38 and I was 39 at the time. A remarkable thing about him was that even when he realized that he was going to die, he would make plans and organize events. He loved the show *Roseanne*, so he would make plans to watch it and tell me and my sister, Lisa, "Bring the kids over and let's have popcorn and watch *Roseanne*," and that's what we did while he was on the couch, very ill. We would do things like that, or watch a concert, or do something musical, or have a picnic in the park. He literally refused to have it all be about dying and he really had a talent for taking the smallest things, like watching *Roseanne*, and make it a fun event. When he became so ill that he had to stay home and be housebound, he created another whole world. Noren and other friends came to visit, his partner came and visited, and different people came to see him, and he always turned these visits into events.

He really didn't do the dying until he truly was near the end. I had to convince him to get into a hospital bed. He was very ill, and he would not get into a hospital bed, I think, because it would have meant admitting that it really was the end, and he didn't want it to be. I had to go to Brainerd and convince him that it was okay to get into that hospital bed. During the last eight weeks he was in hospice, where he fought to live a meaningful life until the end by having conversations and listening to friend's letters from all over the world. At the same time, he began the inward journey of dying, which meant he became quieter.

As he neared the end, he really struggled with the big questions: What is going to happen to me and where am I going? He grappled with the concepts of religion, Christianity, Buddhism, life after death, and wondered what it all meant for him. He believed there was life after death but did not like the rigid boxes around religion that made him feel scorned. He visited often with a Lutheran minister who had personal struggles of his own and reached out to Tim to help him grapple with that which is known and unknown. He loved the concepts of Buddhism and a return to nature.

He had me make a video for his funeral and was very insistent that the different periods of his life be set to very specific music. The parts about Korea were set to Korean music, from tapes he had made himself. Music was important to him, and seemed to be a way for him to come together with people who were present at his funeral or watching the video in some space they had shared.

The video was a bit long for a church funeral—people still remind me of that – but it was what he wanted, and by God, at the end we did what he wanted.

Tim died on February 7, 1993. As he was dying, he was speaking to people in both English and Korean. I asked him, "Who are you talking to?" He was talking to people at a banquet who were all dead. They were Korean people—he told me their names—and people that I knew, like Grandma Warnberg, and they were at a banquet and he said to me, "I want you to come with me." I said, "I can't come with you. This is somewhere that you're going that I can't go."

Keevie and my siblings and parents were there too. We were with him up to the end. When he died, we had all fallen asleep. I think he could not leave when we were awake, and he could feel those connections.

Keevie Fairbanks:

Good memories, but at the same time, sad memories. Like I said, he was a great person and I miss him.

Roxanne Wilson:

He had a lot of courage. He really did transition between worlds, talking to people and going to that banquet. It was a really remarkable, beautiful experience. He was going to be with another set of friends.

I was just reading through his journals and letters, and I found something I'd never seen before, in the final journal he kept. It was on the last page, after a series of blank pages. I think this is one of the last things he wrote, and it has a bit of a religious tone to it. I'm shocked I'd never read it. At the end of his life, he left a message unseen for years that was focused on extending his hospitality by waiting for us at the time of our deaths. It is a comfort to me at 68 years old.

In my most optimistic religious moments I think of Myung-hee (명희), Woo-sun (우선), Yong-bae (용배), Grandpa Warnberg, Grandma Koop, and especially Grandma Warnberg, and I feel joy that I will soon be with them happy and free of pain.

In your most optimistic religious moments, I hope you think of me waiting to welcome you to the wonder of the life beyond the mystery of death.

-Tim Warnberg-

* * *

Tim in His Own Words:

Letter to journalist Terry Anderson, March 20, 1992

(Tim had met Terry Anderson in Kwangju in May 1980, and Anderson had been released three months earlier after more than six years of captivity in Lebanon.)

Dear Terry,

My name is Tim Warnberg and I met you in Kwangju, South Korea nearly twelve years ago when I was a Peace Corp Volunteer and you were reporting on the massacre in that city. My co-worker was Judi Chamberlin and you interviewed me for the Associated Press and taped the interview as well. Robin Moyer, a photographer for Time magazine was also there. I am so happy that after all these years I now at long last have the opportunity to recontact you. I have kept your business card on my desk and thought about you each time there was some snippet of news about the hostages, hoping for your safe release soon. Before going any further, I want to warmly welcome you back to your freedom and your family. Your recent article about your captivity and subsequent release was very moving. Both before and after your forced confinement I have thought about your compassion and kindness when you were reporting on the horror which we witnessed in Kwangju. Your recent poetry and writing reveal that you still have not become jaded and have not been consumed by anger and bitterness but, even in the most depressing of circumstances, have tried to maintain your objectivity and your obvious understanding of and affection for people.

After my Peace Corps experience, I stayed in Korea, studying, and working until 1985. I returned to the United States in 1986 and became a graduate student in Korean literature and language at the University of Hawaii. In 1987 I wrote an article, enclosed with this letter, titled "The Kwangju Uprising: An Inside View," which was published in the *Journal of Korean Studies*. I received my master's and was working on my Ph.D. when I got the devastating news that I have AIDS. I returned home to my family in Minnesota and have somewhat improved, but the disease is slowly taking its toll. I have thought back to the events in my life which have profoundly affected me, and I think of those chaotic days in Kwangju. Not only was I affected by the horror of the massacre and shocked at what humans can do to each other, but, in the midst of catastrophe, I was also impressed with your courage and determination. As a reporter you endeavored to get the truth out, yet you never lost sight of the fact that the stories you were writing were about real people with real emotions. Although people may think that all reporters have these qualities, I realized then that this is definitely not the case.

I hesitate to intrude further on the precious time you are spending with your family but my own situation forces me to be bold: I am wondering if the tape you made of my interview in Kwangju in May 1980 still exists. I don't know what your policy is concerning the tapes you made when you were covering stories but, if possible, I would like to get a copy so that I can listen to my firsthand account of the massacre. If you have taped over the interview or lost the tape I will certainly understand. If that is the case, please accept this letter as a welcome back to "the world" and a wish for much good fortune in your future endeavors.

Sincerely,
Tim Warnberg

Tim Warnberg (March 20)

19. Memories of Tim

by Those Who Knew Him

Paul Courtright:

I met Tim in mid-1979, soon after I was posted to Naju as a Peace Corps Volunteer. Tim was based in Kwangju, right next door to where I lived. In Naju County there were two leprosy resettlement villages, Hohyewon and Hyeonaewon, both of which I was providing support to. These villages were actually closer to Kwangju than the town of Naju was, but they were not close to each other. Hohyewon was the larger of the two, and I felt it was important for me to move to this village in order to better provide for my patients. I was very grateful to Tim when he agreed to help provide support for the other village, Hyeonaewon, from his base in Kwangju.

I moved to Hohyewon in November of 1979. When I got to my village, I realized that the village leader frankly intimidated me. He was impatient with my Korean language skills and he had a very thick South Jeolla accent. Essentially, we were not communicating well.

I was very grateful when Tim agreed to come out to my village in early December and meet with me and my village leader so that we could start a meaningful conversation.

When we met with the village leader, Tim introduced himself, and the leader's response was to ask me "Why can't you speak Korean like him?" I think many of us asked ourselves: "Why can't we speak Korean as well as Tim does?" His Korean was excellent. So, it was great that Tim was there. We had an excellent conversation with my village leader, and we got off onto the right footing in terms of how I was to work and live in my village.

During our meeting, it started snowing. Though huge, fluffy flakes were coming down, Tim and I decided to spend the rest of the day visiting some patients in my community. We laughed at the prospect of visiting people with the snow piling up, and the villagers thought we were absolutely bonkers for being out on a day like that. Tim was happy to be there, as his work in Kwangju was at the university teaching hospital and he did not have as many opportunities to get out into the field. At one of the households their dog had just given birth and they wanted Tim and me to take one or more of the puppies. We just laughed because neither of us were in a position to take care of a dog. So, my first and most important outing with Tim really helped me get started in my communication and my work.

And obviously I am also very grateful to Tim for his hospitality and the hospitality of the ajumeoni at his place in Kwangju where I stayed for several days during the Kwangju Uprising. I certainly wish that Tim were still alive today as he would bring so much to the discussion of what happened in Kwangju and the aftermath.

Tim, we're raising a glass of *soju* or *makgeolli*, toasting you because of the great guy you were, the wonderful work that you did, and for being a good friend.

Tim Warnberg and Paul Courtright at Hohyewon in Naju, 1979.

John Underwood:

John Underwood and his wife, Jean, had worked in Kwangju as missionaries since the late 1960s. Tim Warnberg and Judi Chamberlin had befriended them and visited them often during 5.18. In early June 1980, John Underwood wrote an account of the Kwangju Uprising and gave it to the U.S. Embassy in Seoul. The following paragraph refers specifically to Tim Warnberg's actions in downtown Kwangju on May 18, 1980, when soldiers began unprovoked attacks upon any young men in the vicinity.[16]

---

[16] John Underwood, "Insider's account of Kwangju Riot," 80Seoul 007402, in *May 18 Gwangju Democratization Movement Materials* Vol. 9 (Gwangju: Gwangju City May 18 Historical Materials Compilation Committee, 1997), 363.

Peace Corps volunteers won a good name for Americans at this time by a sort of non-violent intervention. A PCV seeing a person being beaten would go and put their arms around the person, thus being in the way of further beating. On such an occasion the attacker would leave his victim but choose another, who in his turn would be protected by a PCV who put his arms around him.

It is the spontaneous and unanimous opinion of the missionary community living together here that the Peace Corps Volunteers have won a lasting gratitude of great numbers of the citizens of Kwangju for the United States. Sharing the life of the people whom they came to serve, even when it meant sharing serious, perhaps mortal, danger, they made everybody who saw them realize that Americans really care. They identified themselves with the people not by shared animosities but by shared trouble. Missionaries stay as a matter of course, in obedience to a Master and in a bond of love which leaves no choice; but the Peace Corps Volunteers were if anything disobedient to their own master in not leaving the city. It is my personal opinion that if their headquarters had been able to see the situation from the ground as we saw it, headquarters would have hoped that they would stay and do almost exactly what they did. As Americans, we are very proud of our Peace Corps friends.

Lee Heung-cheol:

In 1980, when Mr. Lee was 20, he worked as a DJ at the Tabakne Music Hall in Kwangju, where he first met Tim Warnberg. Lee, who was able to handle broadcasting equipment because he was a DJ, traveled the city in a vehicle and made street-side broadcasts to citizens.

He was interviewed by So Jung-han, a reporter from Ohmynews, for an article published May 12, 2020, titled "The American struck by a soldier's club, the gift he left for Kwangju."

The following is a translation of the article.

It was winter in early 1980, perhaps January. It was then that Tim first came to our music hall. He came and requested a few songs, which I played. He seemed to enjoy it when the songs he requested came on. He asked the waiter to bring me a glass of juice. At that time, what we called juice was just fruit concentrate with water added [laughs]. At any rate, I was grateful to him.

I called him Tim, and he called me Lee. Tim liked Bob Dylan songs, and often requested "Blowin' in The Wind." He also requested Bee Gees songs. I played music for him every time he came, so he often arrived in time for my turn as DJ, perhaps two or three times a week. Later, after we'd gotten to know each other, I let him come into the DJ booth when there weren't many customers.

He had completely adapted to Korean culture. He mostly wore jeans and a shirt and always had a smile on his face. He was friendly and spoke Korean very well, so he was very approachable. He had also completely adapted to Korean food and ate hot or spicy food with no problem. He handled chopsticks perfectly too. We often ate *naengmyeon*, or cold noodles, together. He preferred *bibim-naengmyeon*. I liked spicy food too, so we'd both eat it and I'd ask, "Isn't it spicy?" He always answered, "It's not spicy," even though he kept drinking water.

From the beginning of May [1980], Geumnam-ro and Chungjang-ro had been crowded with students. There were demonstrations every day, so tear gas drifted into the alleys. The music hall was underground and didn't have good ventilation, so neither the customers nor the staff could stay there. As a result, we naturally participated in the demonstrations.

On May 23, I saw Tim near the Provincial Capital. I hadn't seen him in two weeks. And the next morning, we met again by chance in front of the Provincial Capital. He was curious about the situation on the outskirts of Kwangju. I drove him around several neighborhoods as far as the Unam-dong area. He was very surprised to see the situation on the outskirts. I remember he asked, "Have many people died?" and I answered, "Many have died."

It rained that afternoon. It was a drizzling rain that came down in torrents, a hair-raising rain. I was mainly going out and doing street broadcasts, but I came to the Provincial Capital and was in the situation room. Tim came there looking for me. I think it was around 7:30 p.m. It was a little dark. At that time, people in Kwangju trusted foreigners. I think he was let into the provincial capital because he said at the entrance that he was looking for me.

He had something he wanted to talk about and asked me to go outside with him. I was scared for some reason, but I followed him. We walked out by the Provincial Capital annex and went up to the second floor of an inn, where there were six foreign journalists. Tim said, "They're curious about some things, so could you please answer their questions?" I said, "Okay." But then one said he was going to take a photo. I said, "Why are you taking pictures when everyone is now walking around with their faces covered?" I said I was going to leave.

Tim was just barely able to calm me down, and before long, the reporters just started asking me questions. Tim interpreted everything. They asked questions like, "How do you think the situation will proceed in the future?" and "Why did you wear a mask?" Regarding the situation moving ahead, I said, "I really don't know." I explained why I wore a mask, saying, "Who could handle being tracked down and caught?" Helicopters were prowling around at that time, and there were rumors that they were filming everything that moved. The journalists sympathized. When I left the inn after the interview, it was the last time I ever saw Tim.

Terry Anderson:
Terry Anderson was a journalist working for the Associated Press who

spent over a week in Kwangju reporting on the uprising.

I remember Tim well. He was generous with his time and his knowledge and helped us any way he could to tell the story of the Kwangju Uprising. I remember he put me in touch with a Korean pastor who generously allowed us to use his car—our only means other than bicycle to get around. Tim was a kind young man who was justly angry at what he saw. We all liked him.

Robert Grotjohn:

Tim and I both grew up in Brainerd, a small town in central Minnesota, and graduated from the high school in the class of 1973. He was one of the most liked and admired people in our high school, someone who showed kindness and consideration to everyone, so it is no surprise that he was our class president as well as one of the top academic students. We did not become close, however, until we attended the same public liberal arts college, the University of Minnesota at Morris, often exploring the various available alternative consciousnesses together. Eventually, we roomed together for a couple of years. After our sophomore year, Tim helped me get a job at the summer camp where he worked, Camp St. Croix, outside of Hudson, Wisconsin. That was not the last time he found a job for me. I think Tim reached out to many people in many different ways. After university, Tim joined the Peace Corps, and I went back to Brainerd.

Because I knew Tim was in Kwangju, I followed 5.18 closely in the American news media. He was sent home to Minnesota that summer, and he spent a lot of time telling his friends and family about his experiences in Korea, especially his traumatic experiences during May 1980. I remember Tim's horrifying description of a soldier mercilessly beating to death an old woman in the alleyway near where he lived and then pointing his gun at Tim and telling him to go inside or die, and his inspiring description of the taxi drivers' charge on the soldiers at the Provincial Capital building. He told us how he became involved as more than an observer after the first early attacks on Kwangju citizens near the Provincial Capital building. Injured people were lying in the streets, and soldiers prevented anyone from helping them. People asked Tim to help because they believed that the soldiers would not harm a foreigner. He then helped collect and move the wounded to nearby medical facilities.

That summer of 1980, he told me of possible EFL teaching opportunities in Kwangju, as my major was English. He introduced me to the English Department of Chonnam National University in Kwangju, where I taught from March 1981 to June 1984, when I left for graduate school in the United States. While in Korea, I met and married my wife, with whom I have two children and two grandchildren. I taught at two liberal arts colleges in the United States for many years, returned to Korea temporarily on a Fulbright grant in 2009, and returned again in August 2010, this time as Professor of English at Chonnam National University, from which I retired in February 2020.

The point of that autobiographical interjection is that, without Tim as my friend, almost none of my story would have been possible. I think I am not unique in that. He affected almost everyone he met, and he affected most in positive ways. When I first went to Korea, Tim was leading the Kwangju Volunteer Corps, a group of medical students from Chonnam University who would go on Saturdays to a local institution housing mentally challenged people, who were then very neglected in Korean society. The students cleaned the living facilities and engaged the people there in warm human contact, which is what Tim shared with everyone. Tim wrote a letter directly to the Blue House about the deplorable conditions in which those people lived. Jo Namjong, who was an assistant at the Kwangju USIS, helped him to craft the Korean. Once,

Tim and I were walking along Geumnam Street in Kwangju, and a man selling flowers from a street-side kiosk stopped us and invited Tim to a family gathering. The man turned out to be one of the injured people that Tim had helped rescue in the early days of the uprising.

In 2020, *OhmyNews* published several articles about the Peace Corps Volunteers who witnessed the Kwangju Uprising. Two of them focused on Tim's role by investigating the photos of the foreigner helping the injured people, and he is identified as "someone who loved Korea more than Koreans." One of those photos was in the memorial hall of the May 18th National Cemetery when I first visited it in 2004, but it had disappeared when I returned in 2009 and a new hall had been built. The mounted print photos had been replaced with technological wizardry, and Tim almost disappeared from the public-facing record. I am glad that he has received some recognition since, and that his role in 5.18 has reentered the public discourse.

Tim did a lot in his too-short life, and he was poised to do a lot more in the academic world, as he had finished the dissertation that he was never able to defend before he was lost to the AIDS epidemic. I think one of his last trips to Korea was as a translator during the 1988 Olympics, helping introduce a developed Korea with its developing democracy to the world.

Tim was one of the best friends I have ever had. I miss him often. I think it would be a remarkable testament to his time in this world if we knew how many people might say the same about him. I know quite a few of them myself. He was kind, generous, determined, empathetic, and intelligent. He has been visiting my dreams often since I was asked to write this, as he has many times since he passed in 1993. Those dreams give me hope that he is stopped somewhere waiting for us to join him on the other side, in that territory of the unknown country, out ahead of the rest, where he so often was in this world.

Noren Lush:

I was a Peace Corps Volunteer assigned to the Health Clinic in Gimje, in North Jeolla province, while Tim was in South Jeolla province. I didn't get to know Tim until after the Uprising. I was in the Peace Corps office in Seoul for some reason, I think around the end of June or beginning of July 1980, and I saw Tim there. I think he had just returned from a month of R&R back in Minnesota. Later that night we ran into each other at a bar, had a few drinks and ended up talking for hours. We spent all the next day talking as well. The bar we had met in was supposedly a gay bar. I'm gay and Tim was gay, but we had no idea about each other. We were equally shocked to see each other there. It was the first time that either of us had been to a gay bar (a small dive with two sitting rooms and alcohol) and it was the first time that either of us had talked to someone else who was gay. It was a transformative experience and the beginning of a great friendship.

Tim almost never spoke about Kwangju. I figured there was a reason for that, so I didn't push. But eventually I asked, and he told me most of what he would write later in "The Kwangju Uprising: An Inside View," (1987). In addition to what was in the article, Tim also told me about how courageous the citizens of Kwangju were, especially the students and the bus and taxi drivers who drove their vehicles, in formation, to attack military positions.

After our Peace Corps service ended in 1981, we hung out a lot. We both taught at the foreign language school at Yonsei University, and studied Korean there. I also worked at the Royal Asiatic Society and I would drag Tim along on RAS tours that I led or on scouting trips for new tours. In 1985 we both decided to leave Korea for grad school in Hawai'i.

Tim was working on his Ph.D. in Korean literature when he became seriously ill with AIDS. He eventually moved back to Minnesota to be with his family. Tim used his remaining time speaking to various groups about the HIV/AIDS crisis in the United States and discrimination against people suffering from HIV/AIDS.

Tim was a brave man who risked his own safety during the Kwangju Uprising, but it wasn't out of character. Tim was always there for those who needed support—friends, family, strangers—up to the very end of his life.

There's a term in Korean that Koreans invariably used to describe Tim. It sometimes doesn't translate well into English. *Chakhan saram* is often translated as "nice person," or "polite person," or "well-mannered person," but it's more than that. I think that "really good person" comes closest to its true meaning, and that's exactly what Tim was.

Gerry Bevers:

In September 1982, I started Level 3 classes at the Yonsei Korean Language Institute in Seoul. In a Level 6 class, there was a young man about my age who I was told was quite fluent in Korean. When I heard him speak Korean at his graduation ceremony, he seemed pretty fluent to me, especially since I had just finished the Level 3 courses. His name was Tim Warnberg, and he was an ex-Peace Corps Volunteer who was an eyewitness to atrocities committed during the Kwangju Uprising.

I got to talk to Tim before he left to study at the University of Hawaii, but we did not talk about Kwangju because I was more curious to know how he learned to speak Korean so well. I was hoping he could give me some tips on studying the language. I do not remember what he told me, but I do remember being impressed by him, and I remember him being a nice guy. At the time, he was my idol in the sense that I wanted to learn to speak Korean as well as he did.

After Tim left Korea, I never heard any more about him, which surprised me because he had seemed like someone who would have become well-known in the field of Asian Studies.

I searched for him on the internet from time to time, but it was only a few years ago that I discovered he had died at the age of 38. It is sad to realize that someone so full of promise died so young.

Angie Huse:

I was lucky enough to meet Tim Warnberg and a few other Peace Corps volunteers when my family lived in Seoul between 1980 and 1982. It was there that I met Cornie Choy, who was from Hawaii and who lived and worked in Korea for 17 years. Cornie loved the country and wanted others to also see it as he did. He wanted to introduce people to the beautiful countryside, the peaceful temples, the varied regional foods, and the wonderful Korean people who worked hard and played harder. To do this, Cornie organized something called the Korea Art Club, which was affiliated with the Royal Asiatic Society. He took groups on trips outside Seoul to explore some little-known part of the peninsula and always tried to contact the Peace Corps Volunteers who lived and worked in those areas to see if they could help out, since they had language skills and specialized knowledge of the areas they lived and worked in.

It was on one of these trips that I met Tim, and Noren Lush as well. After that, whenever Tim came to Seoul, he would try to visit us for a meal or a concert. My children were very fond of their "uncles," who were younger and definitely more fun than their old parents. Once Tim and Noren spent a long summer's weekend with us at Daejon Beach where we cooked and swam and ate and had so much fun. I will always remember him that way.

Once we got to know him, he spoke to us about his personal experience in Kwangju, but we had to be a little circumspect then about what we talked about and to whom, so I am sure we did not get all the details. He did tell us that the number of casualties reported by the authorities was far too small.

I got to know Tim well enough that he came out to me. The climate of acceptance and opinion was so different in 1982, and I think even among some of the PCVs in Korea, attitudes changed after Tim told them of who he really was. It was not something you divulged so casually then. I feel honored that he thought enough of me to tell me and trusted that my attitude toward him would not change.

It was only a decade ago that I learned of Tim's passing, but I was cheered to learn that Tim was in his hometown when he died. I knew his father was the sheriff there and I met him briefly when he visited Seoul. Tim told me he had not been able to tell his family, except for one sister, of his sexual orientation. I think Tim thought a lot of his father and was always concerned that he might be a disappointment to him. Learning that he died where he was born means that all the issues he was concerned with must have been resolved and that his family knew and accepted him for who he was. And for that I am glad.

Susan Cunningham-Jopling (Woo Soon-jin):

The story of eight months spent with my teacher and friend, Tim Warnberg, begins at Kamp Kimchee, a week-long camp for Korean adoptees and their families to learn about their cultural heritage. The camp offers classes in Korean language, art, taekwondo, and Korean dance.

I taught at Kamp Kimchee for six years, focusing on building self-esteem in the children. My primary mission was to teach kids to feel okay being Korean in a predominantly Caucasian society. I taught from firsthand knowledge, recalling how I struggled with everyday life during my childhood, not having parents that looked like me, and especially the struggle of trying to fit in.

It was a typical, hot July day and the camp was in full swing. My class had ended, and I was putting the students' things away, when in he walked.

"Hi, I'm Tim Warnberg, you must be Susan!" he said, greeting me in a gentle, non-threatening voice.

We spoke of life in Korea, and I told Tim about my upcoming trip, which involved a tour by the orphanage through which I had been adopted. What timing, because here was Tim and he was willing to share all he knew and advise me on what I could expect on my trip there. It was like having a living Korean guidebook at my fingertips! Tim was able to help me prepare for the tour unlike anyone or anything else could. With his ten years of experiences there, and his willingness to prepare me for all I would encounter, I felt more secure that my journey would be one of self-discovery beyond the typical tourist sightseeing trip. I felt I was already halfway there, though my pilgrimage was yet to begin.

Tim was well versed in the plight of new adoptees, having worked in Korea with orphanages and escorted children to America for adoption. This usually involved 10 to 20 children at a time. Tim's father once told me, pride in his voice, "Tim would board the plane and ask if anyone was willing to take a child and help him on the long flight to America. Not one person would ever refuse or say no and not help him."

Tim told me that one of the hardest times he ever had was escorting a little girl who had bonded with him because he only spoke to her in Korean during the 15-hour-long flight. When they got to the airport, Tim said, "It tore my heart apart," because he had to hand over this little girl to an American family who "spoke not a word of Korean." The little girl kept screaming and crying. In Korean she pleaded, "*Oppa! Oppa, ANIYO! Jebal, gajimaseyo!*" (Older brother, older brother, NO! Please, don't go!)

Tim gave me some background about himself, saying he had lived in Korea for ten years. He added that he looked forward to sharing his Korean experience with me, because it meant little to everyone else, but he suspected I might be interested.

At the time of my introduction to Tim, I had been taking Korean language classes to learn as much as I could about my culture. We talked briefly about my Korean language teacher, Mrs. Park, and how she had given him my phone number. Mrs. Park had met Tim through an acquaintance, and she gave him my phone number because she felt our meeting would be rewarding for both of us.

During his stay in Korea, Tim made many friends. I had the great fortune to meet one friend, Lee Jung-tae, during my trip to Korea in 1992. He lived in Seoul with his wife and two daughters. Upon arrival in Seoul, I called Jung-tae at the number Tim had provided. By having known Tim, Jung-tae could take me to places that they loved to visit.

I have tried throughout my life to find my roots, including searching for my birth family, and to seek answers to many other questions that arise from being adopted. I feel strongly that this is why Tim and I were destined to meet, despite being from different parts of the world. I was full of questions about many missing fragments of my life, and he was full of knowledge and potential to help me answer these questions.

I had the pleasure of inviting Tim to Kamp Kimchee, and Tim spoke to a recent adoptee in Korean. She just looked wide-eyed at him and didn't say a word. Tim said many adoptees lose their language because they do not have anyone to speak with in Korean. As well, they choose not to speak for fear of not fitting in, Tim said.

I have lived the pain of the adopted child from Korea, and I know that even if other adoptees choose not to acknowledge it in their own lives, it is something that will always be there. It's something that is undeniable.

But knowledge, particularly knowledge combined with cultural sensitivity, helps a great deal. Tim answered so many of my questions. From his experiences with Korean adopted children, he was able to see adoption from the viewpoint of the adoptee, rather than from the perspective of the adoptive parents. He truly was a bridge, anchored as he was with a foot planted firmly in each culture. Listening to his perspective was like giving adopted children a voice to express how and what they felt but couldn't put into words. Tim, having the knowledge of the Korean way of thinking, could put the two worlds together in a way that I could understand.

The time I spent with Tim was beyond my expectations. We used to take long walks and talk about everything under the sun. It was such a gift and great way to get to know him. Finding Tim was like finding my birth family and losing him was like losing them.

Tim is no longer with us, but he made a lasting impression on my life that I want to carry with me forever. I was given the opportunity to spend eight glorious months getting to know a side of Tim few people had the chance of knowing.

I once asked my Korean teacher, "Why Tim, why me, and why did you give him my phone number?" She said it was simply because she thought we would become good friends. He became a friend yes, but a teacher and mentor too, and I know I gained something more than friendship that will last a lifetime. I gained the opportunity to be the last to cross that bridge Tim created between the two cultures that dwell within myself.

I dedicate this in memory of Tim Warnberg, who enriched my life beyond words.

A poem I wrote in Tim's honor:

Precious is someone of great value, highly esteemed or cherished.
Precious is how I feel about our friendship.
Precious is what you have taught me about life.
Precious is the love you hold in your heart and give to me so freely.
This is you, Tim, and what you mean to me
Precious

20. The Kwangju Uprising: An Inside View

Tim Warnberg

The Kwangju Incident of May 1980, although one of the crucial events in the post-Korean War history of South Korea, remains a subject of great controversy and confusion. A variety of contradictory accounts and analyses of the incident have appeared, but a day-by-day recounting of the uprising, drawn from previously unpublished eyewitness accounts, contradicts both the official government report and many of the contemporary press accounts. The experiences of eyewitnesses, including Peace Corps volunteers and resident missionaries, suggest that the events in Kwangju represented an indigenous, immediate response to military and police violence, rather than a planned provocation manipulated by outside political forces. The incompatibility of these eyewitness accounts with the Korean government report, as well as the reluctance of the government to respond at all, reflects a lack of clarity surrounding the Kwangju incident which will ensure its continuing impact on the contemporary political scene in Korea, and establishes the need for an even-handed report and analysis of the incident incorporating all available information and accounts.

On May 18, 1980, what began as a small and, by Korean standards, relatively routine demonstration in the city of Kwangju, population 800,000, Cholla province, developed into a violent confrontation with the military which resulted in a large number of civilian and military deaths and caused repercussions that are still evident on the political scene today. Since that time a number of attempts have been made to clarify exactly what occurred and why. The official version put forth by the Korean government is decidedly different from versions published by a number of human rights groups in and out of Korea. As a Peace Corps volunteer (PCV) in the city of Kwangju who witnessed the uprising, I will present an account of the incident based on previously unpublished eyewitness reports which may contribute to a better understanding of the events that transpired. Although in previous reports the number of deaths is one of the main points of contention, the focus and intent of this article will not be to take sides in that dispute. Rather, through eyewitness accounts, I will present a picture of the initial confrontation and subsequent events that eventually led to a full-scale armed revolt, and I will compare these accounts with the official government version and press reports. In light of their continuing impact on Korea today, there remains a need for a discussion of the events and of the government's handling of the situation.

Background to the Uprising

Two factors played an important role in the Kwangju uprising. The first is regionalism. The Korean landscape is remarkable for the many mountain ranges that crisscross and divide the countryside. Kyongsang and Cholla Provinces, two major regions in South Korea, are bisected and separated by one such mountain range. By making travel difficult and impeding social and economic intercourse, the mountains have helped to foster and preserve a regionalism that the introduction of modern communications has only recently begun to alleviate.

Regionalism in Korea has its origins in the Three Kingdoms period, when Cholla was part of the kingdom called Paekche and Kyongsang was part of the Silla kingdom.[1] After centuries of internecine wars, the peninsula was finally united in the tenth century under the tutelage of the Koryo dynasty. Koryo began a pattern of discrimination against the Paekche region by assimilating the ruling aristocratic class of Silla, which had peacefully surrendered, into its governing structure while using much harsher methods to subjugate Paekche, which had resisted integration to the end. In the sixteenth and seventeenth centuries, regionalism played a role in the groupings and regroupings of the literati factions, and in more recent times, evidence of regionalism can be found in the loyalties of the communist and nationalist movements.[2] As a result of these geographical and historical factors, Cholla and Kyongsang have developed rather distinct dialects and characteristics.

In modern Korea, this regionalism still flares up and is manifested in its better form in good-natured but heated athletic rivalries. More serious social manifestations can be seen in the reluctance of the people from the two regions to intermarry. Koreans throughout the nation have very strong stereotypes regarding the people from these two areas. Kyongsang people are described variously as loyal, aloof, cliquish, manly, stubborn, and rough in manner and language. Cholla people are frequently called two-faced, conniving, uncooperative, brutish, opportunistic, and uncouth, as well as intelligent and artistic.[3] Although the rivalry between the two provinces is usually good-natured and cordial, in extraordinary circumstances this mutual distrust can turn ugly. In addition, these strong regional sentiments are further aggravated by the fact that the nation's political power rests with a clique that for the last twenty-six years has been drawn largely from Kyongsang Province (presidents Park and Chun), while the most prominent opposition leader of the last fifteen years is from Cholla Province (Kim Dae Jung).

The second important underlying consideration in any analysis of the events of that May is the political situation in the months preceding the Kwangju Incident. The generally confrontational political scene in Korea had become even more so in the latter half of 1979 and through the early months of 1980. With the rise of Kim Yŏng-sam as leader of the New Democratic Party and his dramatic and unexpected (by the ruling party) victory as head of the opposition,[4] the stage was set for the events of the next twelve months. When the ruling party, charging him with "antistate remarks," forcibly expelled Kim from his seat in the National Assembly on October 5, 1979,[5] it set off a chain of events that had such a drastic impact on the Korean political scene that it is still being felt today. On the day of his ouster Kim himself predicted, "In the not too distant future, this crime will receive the judgement of the people."[6]

Following Kim's ouster there was a series of violent antigovernment demonstrations in Pusan and Masan, two cities in Kim's home province of Kyongsang, that resulted in the government declaring limited martial law.[7] In the ensuing debate over how to deal with the rising popular support for the antigovernment movement, Kim Chae-kyu, head of the Korean Central Intelligence Agency (KCIA), took matters into his own hands and assassinated his longtime superior, President Park Chung Hee, on October 26, 1979. In the following day's paper a small picture of General Chun Du Hwan appeared, identifying him as the officer in charge of the investigation of the assassination.[8] Within two months Chun arrived at the conclusion that Army Chief of Staff and Martial Law Commander Chong Sung-hwa was implicated in Park's death and on December 12, 1979, he moved against him in what has come to be known as the 12/12 Incident.[9] Chun used his Capital Garrison Command and troops commanded by classmates from the Korea Military Academy, including new President Roh Tae-woo, to overpower the marine units defending General Chŏng. Chong was arrested and convicted. The American ambassador to Korea, William Gleysteen, cabled Washington that "Park loyalists opposed to political liberalization have staged a coup."[10]

Nevertheless, following the 12/12 Incident there was a definite move toward liberalization. The far-reaching emergency decrees of the Yusin constitution[11] were dismantled, students were released, and opposition leaders had their civil rights restored, including the perennial opposition leader Kim Dae Jung. The atmosphere in Korea in early 1980 was one of guarded optimism; people openly discussed Korea's political future and debated the merits of the three undeclared candidates in the promised presidential elections,[12] the so-called three

Kims—Kim Yŏng-sam, Kim Dae Jung, and Kim Jong-pil.[13] General Chun, meanwhile, continued to consolidate his own power and by April 1980 was head of the Korean CIA and military intelligence.[14] The students were becoming increasingly restless and vocal, and by April were demanding an immediate end to martial law and the removal of Chun, who was widely believed to be the power behind acting-president Ch'oe Kyu-ha.

Throughout April and into early May demonstrations increased in scope, number, and degree of violence. On May 15, approximately one-hundred thousand students demonstrated in the streets of Seoul, as the students had set noon the previous day as the deadline for the end of martial law. Though eyewitness accounts generally agree that the demonstration was peaceful at first, it quickly degenerated into violence and finally resulted in the death of a policeman when a bus was commandeered and driven into police lines.[15]

Friday, May 16, and Saturday, May 17, were relatively calm, as the student leaders had agreed to call off street demonstrations.[16] Meanwhile, sometime in the week prior to May 18, the military had apparently decided to make their move. On May 16, Dr. and Mrs. Betts Huntley, missionaries in Kwangju affiliated with Kwangju Christian Hospital, reported that they were unable to buy bus tickets to Taejŏn because the army had bought the entire supply. They took the train instead, only to find a train and a station packed with soldiers. They later learned that the troops were being moved around the country in preparation for the declaration of martial law at midnight Saturday, May 17.[17]

Keeping this volatile political situation in mind, as well as the latent regional hostility, let us now turn to the events of May 18, 1980. In Korea, important events are remembered by their dates and 5/18 has come to symbolize what is known as the Kwangju Incident. What follows is a day by day recounting of what happened from May 18 to May 27, drawn entirely from the personal accounts, including my own, of Peace Corps volunteers who witnessed all or part of the incident, and other accounts from several American missionaries who were living in Kwangju at the time.

Daily Account of the Kwangju Incident

Once the uprising was underway, it was really difficult to know what was happening, who was in control, and which rumors were true and which were not. One thing, however, was clear: most people witnessed enough brute force initially to automatically believe everything they heard. All rumors were assumed to be true. Throughout the ten days the prevailing mood was one of apprehension; everyone wondered what was going to happen and what was going on at any given moment throughout the city. That the situation eventually became an acute

Kwangju City--Downtown

To
Chŏnnam
University

To
Chosŏn
Univ

To
Chŏnnam U
Hospital

1. Provincial Capitol
2. Samu Kwan
3. Ch'oe Il Building
4. Catholic Center
5. Bank of Kwangju

6. Tourist Hotel
7. Post Office
8. Student Union
9. American Cultural Center
10. Bus Terminal

political and social crisis is an undeniable fact, but the reasons for the spiral into violence remain obscure or overlooked. For a better understanding of the incident's origins I will pay particularly close attention to the events of the first few days. Those events are crucial, both to the government's justification for its subsequent actions as well as to the people's justification for their eventual active armed resistance.

Sunday, May 18. In the early morning hours Kim Dae Jung, Kim Jong-pil, officers of student groups, and nationwide leaders of the movement for democracy were arrested.[18] Several Peace Corps volunteers, who had come to Kwangju from their villages for the weekend, gathered at the Kwangju Tourist Hotel and discussed the declaration of martial law the previous evening. At the hotel we met with David Miller of the American Cultural Center, but he had no useful information. At around 11 A.M. we went out into Kwangju's main thoroughfare, Kŭmnam Street, and proceeded toward the city bus terminal (see map). When we had only gone one block, we saw a gathering of students, numbering about thirty, form a group, somewhat tentatively at first, and march down the middle of the street, demanding the release of Kim Dae Jung and all arrested students and the lifting of martial law. They had marched no farther than one block when they were met by a line of combat police and an Armored Personnel Carrier.[19] The combat police had been stationed at the Samu Kwan, the local army reserve building, half a block away.

The students took stones from a nearby construction site and hurled them at the police, who immediately responded with tear gas. The official government report states that "at 11:50 A.M. about two hundred students from Chŏnnam University confronted police, exchanging tear gas and stones as they tried to march into the heart of the city."[20] This must refer to a different group from the one we witnessed, because we were already in the heart of the city and initially there were only about thirty students involved. Therefore, the confrontation we witnessed was likely the first encounter also to be witnessed by a large number of Kwangju's citizens.

On any Sunday in Kwangju many families go downtown to attend church or go shopping, so the streets are always full of ordinary citizens. Running parallel to the main street is a five-block promenade, somewhat like a large outdoor mall, which is always packed with people shopping, sightseeing, selling their wares, or just out for a stroll. Though the cannisters were not directed at them, due to their proximity to the students, it was this crowd that was soon enveloped in tear gas. Each time a cannister was fired the crowd grew larger and angrier. At one point, we witnessed a policeman taunt the crowd by running out of the police line and shaking his fist, as if daring the crowd to throw stones. Throw stones they did, and the combat police responded by shooting more tear gas cannisters and throwing the stones back. Traffic was disrupted, further swelling the crowded downtown streets, as people could not take buses out of the area. For several hours, the crowd played cat and mouse with the combat police, but the initial violence did not seem serious compared to the many other demonstrations we had previously witnessed in Seoul.

At around 3 P.M. I looked behind me and saw that the airborne paratroopers[21] had arrived and were blocking passage down Kumnam Street. At precisely that moment the soldiers charged and began swinging their clubs. We ran with the panicked crowd and I ended up in a small store along with about fifteen other people, including one other PCV. A soldier came into the store and proceeded to club everyone over the head with his truncheon until he came to the other volunteer and me. He stopped, startled, hesitated a moment, and then ran out. We went out into the side street and found that the troops had retreated to the main street, leaving behind wounded people everywhere. Most of the injured had suffered serious blows to the head, arms, or legs. Two volunteers and I picked up a delivery boy for a Chinese restaurant who had been knocked off his bike by a blow to the head. We brought him to a clinic and managed to convince the reluctant doctor to open his door. He said he feared retaliation from the military.

Other wounded people filled the streets and tried to push their way in, but he only let in about ten people before he locked the door again. People banged on the door cursing and screaming. One young boy, bleeding from a gash on his forehead, told us he had been playing billiards when the paratroopers burst in and beat each person sharply on the head and then withdrew. The others had similar stories—though some were actively demonstrating, many were simply attending to their business when the troops indiscriminately began to beat them.

We left the clinic and encountered bruised, battered, and beaten people wherever we went. The other volunteers decided to return to their villages, so they made their way to the local bus terminal. I started for home and found another group of soldiers savagely and randomly beating young men in the street across from my house.

Martha Huntley, a missionary who had lived in Kwangju for nearly fifteen years, relates the following:

We took a bus back to Kwangju from Taejŏn on Sunday morning, the 18th. As we came by taxi in from the bus station, the driver took a very circuitous route. We asked him why he was going that way and he said that there was some trouble in the streets downtown. Shortly after we arrived home, around noon, the telephone began ringing and didn't cease for days as various friends and students of ours called to say they were being attacked in the streets, beaten, kicked, and so on, or their friends and relatives were. Many called to describe what was happening on their street as they looked out the window.

No one knew what was going on. They wanted to know if we knew anything about it, if the American Cultural Center people knew, if the State Department knew. Many of the people on the streets of Kwangju on Sunday morning were going to church or taking their children to Sunday school, so a high percentage of the attacked were Christians.

One man we knew, a businessman about thirty, was pulled off the bus he was riding (along with other youngish-looking people), and was kicked about the head so bad he lost an eye. Another young mother about the same age, thirty or early thirties, who was taking her two children to Sunday school, was beaten and left unconscious on the sidewalk—she had to have stitches in her scalp and was incoherent for four months—her husband joined the students Sunday afternoon when they fought with the soldiers. No one knew what was happening or why.

That night I stood on the roof of my house and looked out over Kwangju. A burning truck could be seen in the direction of the railroad station, but the city seemed relatively calm.

Monday, May 19. As I went to work at about 11:30 A.M., I found a large crowd of people in front of the Catholic Center on Kŭmnam Street. Because the demonstration was in the center of the city, it was difficult to say who was demonstrating and who was there on legitimate business. At any rate, there was a large crowd gathered and they had apparently just stoned the center, where it was rumored the Martial Law Command had set up a post. Some people were chanting antigovernment slogans, and a burning car was in the middle of the street. At that point it appeared that the number of people actively demonstrating was relatively small. Many more people, however, lined the streets and were hanging out of buildings to see what was going on. The paratroopers, stationed around the nearby capitol building, suddenly attacked the crowd and began to beat people with their truncheons. In the ensuing panic, a middle-aged housewife screamed to me for help as a soldier tried to wrest her teenage son away. I managed to convince the soldier to let the boy go, but not until he rapped the boy on the head and struck me across the face with his club. As I walked away with the woman, she kept asking hysterically, "What's happening? Why are they doing this?"

After circling around some back alleys, I returned to the main street. A Korean doctor approached me and asked if I would help carry the wounded to his clinic. The soldiers had sealed off the streets and forced all of the wounded to sit in the middle of the street, some of them badly injured. Most of the victims had been clubbed, although some of the injuries may have been due to the crush of the panicked mob. We pushed our way through the troops and were able to take some of the worst cases to the clinic. After several trips the soldiers refused to let us through. The remaining thirty or so injured were forced to run a gauntlet to the back of a military truck and climb in under their own power. It was at this point that I began to hear murmurs from the crowd—Let's

245

rise up! Let's fight!—not from students, but from ordinary people in the streets.

The doctor and I, carrying a severely wounded man on a stretcher, managed to push past the soldiers and get to Chŏnnam University Hospital, where I worked. The doctors told us that they had already received a large number of wounded on Sunday, more were coming in, and one middle-aged man was on the verge of death from concussion. The man I carried to the hospital was the owner of a small flower shop in front of the Catholic Center. To illustrate the seriousness of the blow he received to his head, when I met him again two years and eleven operations later, he was still unable to speak.

Judi Chamberlin, another PCV, and I left the hospital to take an orphan to the Chŏnju Hospital for ear surgery. It was around one o'clock. We took a city bus and were about two blocks from the terminal when we were stopped by a column of soldiers. We forced our way off the bus and tried to take back roads to the station. The soldiers were in riot gear and were walking through back alleys in residential areas, selecting young men, many of them standing alone in front of their shops or houses, and beating them on their heads and arms. We tried to stop them but were pushed away.

Other Peace Corps volunteers reported that the bus terminals were chaotic with soldiers charging in, separating out the young men, and beating and detaining them.[22]

Tuesday, May 20. The morning was quite calm, if uneasy, and I made my way to work without incident. After lunch, another volunteer and I were taking a city bus to the local terminal when paratroopers blocked the road. We managed to get off the bus and onto a residential sidestreet just as the soldiers began to move into the crowd and hit all the young men viciously around the head. When I confronted a military commander, he said, "It doesn't matter how many get killed." The missionaries, who are affiliated with a local hospital, reported that they began to receive the wounded Sunday afternoon and Monday morning, and by Tuesday every effort was being made not to admit people except for the seriously wounded, because so many were coming in with contusions, abrasions, broken arms, and so on.[23] I left town Tuesday afternoon and did not see what transpired, but upon my return the next afternoon, I discovered that the Korean Broadcasting System (KBS) and Munhwa Broadcasting Company (MBC), the Korean television stations, had been forced off the air by mobs angry at what they felt was incorrect and biased reporting of the previous day's events. Rumors concerning the use of troops from Kyŏngsang Province were rampant.

Wednesday, May 21. On Wednesday morning another PCV and I tried to go back to Kwangju, but found that bus service had been discontinued. We hitchhiked and walked, arriving in the city around 2 P.M. As we walked into the city, we had to go through a line of soldiers, not paratroopers, standing in formation across the highway which leads into Kwangju from the southern suburb of Songjongni. Once we reached the city limits, it was obvious that something incredible had transpired in our absence. The streets were crowded and citizens were patrolling them in commandeered buses and trucks. Most of the passengers were armed with M-1s. We learned that early Wednesday morning the people had engaged the army in a widespread revolt, commandeering buses, military jeeps, and Armored Personnel Carriers, and raiding ammunition dumps to secure carbines, M-1 rifles, pistols, and thousands of rounds of ammunition. The missionaries and other PCVs agreed that around 1 or 2 P.M. the military had begun firing on the demonstrators.[24] By the time I arrived on foot from the outskirts of town at 4 P.M., there was a serious gunbattle on Kŭmnam Street. Kwangju Christian Hospital reported that in the hours from two to four they received ninety-nine severely wounded patients, and fourteen dead.[25] We watched the fighting on the main street and then walked around the local medical clinics, checking on the wounded. Most had gunshot wounds, but several had been bayonetted. Later that day some students set up a machine gun on the roof of Chŏnnam University Hospital, and the army made the decision to withdraw to the outskirts of the city.

Thursday, May 22. Since the army had withdrawn, the city was relatively quiet, but there was still much confusion. We went to the Chŏnnam University Hospital morgue and counted twenty-seven bodies. An English and a Danish reporter decided to tag along so we could translate. Everywhere we went people crowded around and tried to tell us what they had seen. People were particularly incensed that the local news media was distorting the truth so much; they wanted to make sure that the world knew of their plight. We went to the Christian Hospital and talked to a wounded student, who claimed that he was one of a group of students from Seoul National University who had tried to come into Kwangju from the nearby hamlet of Tamyang and had been fired upon by troops. He thought that he was probably the only survivor of a group of thirty.

That afternoon the citizens formed a group called the "May 18th Coordinating Committee of 15," and went to negotiate at the military headquarters in Sangmudae. The seven demands presented were: 1) no more deployment of combat forces; 2) acknowledgement by the military of its excesses in the suppression of opposition in Kwangju; 3) the release of all students and youths held in detention; 4) proper compensation for the deceased and wounded; 5) no blame should be placed on the citizens; 6) the military should not retaliate once the situation was settled; and 7) all demands should be broadcast by radio to the entire nation.[26] Late in the afternoon about thirty to fifty thousand people gathered in front of the Provincial Capitol building and a debate ensued as to which demands should be pursued. There was a scuffle on the platform and it was difficult to know who stood for what. Although some leaders argued against any of the political demands and for surrendering arms, the majority of the people at the rally clearly wanted to fight until the military accepted all the demands. As we stood watching the argument on the makeshift stage set up in front of the capitol, a man suspected of spying for the government was brought through the crowd. He would have been torn to pieces on the spot if his student bodyguards had not zealously protected him. People spit at him, yelled obscenities, and tried to kick and punch him. By the end of the day the makeup of the committee representing the people of Kwangju had changed, and we later learned that those opposed to compromise had prevailed.

Friday, May 23. Things calmed down considerably, with the students organizing clean-up crews, and gun collection and registration. A plane flew over early in the morning and dropped leaflets which said that the authorities knew that outside agitators were responsible, not the good citizens of Kwangju. These leaflets, as well as the increasingly biased and incorrect reporting on TV and radio served to intensify the local feelings of isolation and anger.

A new coordinating committee of students and citizens, as well as a "struggle committee," were set up to take the place of the disbanded group of the previous day. We met with reporters from *Time* (Robin Moyer) and AP (Terry Anderson), and gave an account of what we had seen. We got caught out after curfew and spent the night with reporters in a small inn behind the Provincial Capitol. At one point a young man came to our room and attempted to explain the students' position, but he was so incoherent from lack of sleep that he finally gave up and went out. That night the number of vehicles on the streets, as well as the number of shots heard, was greatly diminished.

Saturday, May 24. We accompanied Robin Moyer and some German reporters to the Provincial Capitol building, where we were given passes and allowed inside. It was difficult to ascertain who was representing the views of the committee that had been set up the previous day. Many people were eager to talk to the foreign press, but no one seemed to have a clear idea of what direction to take, now that they had succeeded in driving the soldiers out of the city. There was a news conference from which Korean journalists were pointedly excluded, because the students were angry at the inaccurate reports appearing in the domestic press. I talked to a reporter from the *Dong-A Daily News* who was very upset; he claimed that he was sending accurate reports, but they were being censored in Seoul.

We met a student from Chŏnnam National University who was convinced that the army would come back into the city soon. He was a young man who wanted to make it clear that many of the students felt that they had been forced by the military to defend themselves with arms. As he put it, "Could we just sit by and do nothing while our neighbors and friends were being beaten and killed before our eyes?" He wanted to make sure that the foreign press realized that this was not a political movement, though there were, he felt, legitimate political demands, but rather an attempt by the people of Kwangju to defend themselves from what they perceived to be the arbitrary use of military force. That was a theme we heard repeatedly from people who came up to us on the street to tell their stories.

After about an hour we left the capitol and went to Chonnam University Hospital. Beds lined the entrance and corridors. Though none of the doctors wanted to be quoted or officially interviewed, they were very anxious to show us the wounded and dead, and gave us free reign to wander about. We went to the temporary morgue behind the hospital and counted about thirty bodies.[27] Hundreds of people milled around, screaming when they discovered a relative or friend among the victims. We then walked to the Samu Kwan across from the Provincial Capitol, where another temporary morgue had been set up by students. There we counted over one hundred bodies. Late in the afternoon, a rally was held in front of the capitol and Chun Du Hwan was burned in effigy. The size of the crowd was about fifty thousand. That night, at three-thirty A.M., we heard heavy shooting and thought the army was moving back into the city, but we awoke to an unchanged situation.

Sunday, May 25. A relatively quiet day, though tensions were running very high. News releases from Seoul were reporting widespread looting and severe shortages, though we never met anyone in the city making such complaints. Several students in the capital building had been stabbed in the backs of their legs with ballpoint pens by unknown assailants, and the prevailing feeling was that the government was trying to create chaos as an excuse to move back into the city. The next day's paper reported, "one of the students fell to the ground and the other sucked poison out of his colleague's wound and he also collapsed the next moment. Both are in critical condition."[28] Since I knew one of the students who had been stabbed, I went to the hospital to see him. He was only suffering from fatigue and really did not seem to know what had happened, except that he had been stabbed from behind. The attending doctor said it was not serious, that the fluid was only ink.

We attended a rally in the center of the city and it was announced that bus service would resume. An angry group of people confronted us, demanding to know if General Wickham[29] had authorized the use of troops to put down the people of Kwangju. We managed to convince them that we truly knew nothing about it.

Monday, May 26. Judi Chamberlin and I attended a meeting with the missionaries about plans for foreigners to evacuate the city. They had received word that all foreigners were to leave Kwangju. We decided along with them that it would be best to stay. According to Martha Huntley:

A nurse from the Christian Hospital came to their house on the morning of May 26 and introduced a young woman as "Mrs. Kim," saying that she had come to visit her and got trapped in the city when it was closed off. Early that morning someone had murdered all the people in the house next door, so they wondered if Mrs. Kim could stay with the missionaries. Mrs. Huntley agreed. Within an hour the phone rang and it was from Seoul; this was very strange since phone service to Kwangju had been cut off one week earlier. It was the Blue House.[30] It turned out that Mrs. Kim was a relative of President Ch'oe Kyu-ha. The Blue House called several times a day to ask about her welfare. Mrs. Kim insisted that Ch'oe was surrounded by people who did not want him to know what was going on and her life would be in danger from them if she tried to get any real information to him. Both her husband and her brother were on the Blue House staff and she herself worked for an American military hospital. Eventually she was taken out of Kwangju by helicopter.

That afternoon we attended a mass funeral service held at the Samu Kwan. We counted about forty caskets. After the service we walked over to the Provincial Capitol, where we counted another twenty unclaimed bodies. Late in the afternoon we met with Henry Scott Stokes of the *New York Times*. He told us that the American government had convinced the Koreans not to bomb the city. I walked to the hospital where I worked and talked to one of the doctors from the Dermatology Department. He had been on assignment at the military hospital on the edge of town, and reported seeing fifty bodies airlifted from the military hospital morgue in a one hour period. That night, rumors that the army was planning on retaking the city were rampant. People were jittery.

Tuesday, May 27. Judi Chamberlin, Dave Dolinger, and I awoke at about 3 A.M., when the army began moving in with tanks and percussion bombs. A woman's voice over a loudspeaker pleaded for people to come to the Provincial Capitol and defend themselves. We listened to her desperate pleas for at least an hour until she was finally silenced by gunfire. By 5:30 A.M. there were troops directly beneath our second-story room, and we went out on the veranda and watched them go from house to house trying to flush out suspected "rebels." They were regular army troops and wore white armbands. At 8:30 we went out into the city. There were pools of blood along the streets, as well as tanks and soldiers. We counted fifteen bodies.[31] One soldier told us that they had been told that there was a communist insurrection that had to be put down. We walked to the capitol. The left side of the building had been gutted and was riddled with bullets. The half-burnt body of a student we had talked to a few days earlier was lying in a second-story windowwell.

The soldiers were hog-tying the captured with wire, lining them up, and kicking them in their heads. An enraged reporter from *ABC News* put his camera down and attempted to intervene, but other soldiers pulled him off. We went to talk to reporters who had witnessed the assault. They showed us bullet holes in the walls of their rooms, and said they had been fired upon as a warning not to photograph the event. All through the day and into the night groups of soldiers roamed the streets, searching for people and leading them away from inns, homes, and shops. People were warned not to harbor any suspected rebels. The Kwangju Uprising was over.

Reporting

According to the Korean government, 191 people lost their lives during the Kwangju Uprising. Other sources report from 300 to 2,000 deaths.[32] Whatever the correct figures, it is obvious that perceptions of the incident, in Korea as well as abroad, vary widely. A brief review of the reporting on the Kwangju Uprising by North and South Korea, China, and the Soviet Union reveals a wide disparity in accounts.

The Soviet Union's reporting of the uprising tends to parrot that of North Korea, although it is not as dramatic. The event is portrayed in revolutionary terms, using such phrases as "employees and workers marched shoulder to shoulder with students."[33] They blame the uprising on severe repression by the ruling regime, but they appear to have saved their most serious barbs for the United States, reporting "Washington is directly responsible for the Kwangju tragedy."[34]

Soviet accounts also take the opportunity to chastise the Chinese: "Chinese hegemonists are acquiescing to U.S. moves."[35] The overall report, however, was fairly accurate concerning facts and figures. The Soviets, it seems, were much more interested in blasting U.S. policies than in commenting on the South Korean government's suppression of the uprising.

The Chinese, too, followed the North Korean line, but interestingly enough did not denounce the United States or American policies in Korea. Any criticism of the U.S. was always indirect and attributed either to North Korea or the foreign press. They also tried to portray the uprising as socialist in nature, by using pregnant phrases such as "thousands of peasants flocked in from the countryside, including miners with explosives."[36] Their denunciations and criticisms were more indirect, and they left the final chapter to history: "This murder of the people by the South Korean fascists will be subject to history's harsh judgement."[37]

North Korean response and reporting up until May 29 were fairly accurate (and thus it appears that the corresponding Soviet and Chinese accounts were also quite accurate). At times they engaged in histrionics—"demonstrators were clubbed till the streets were dyed with blood"[38]—and exaggerated the role of workers, miners, and peasants, but generally the initial reporting of the events was quite accurate.

On May 19, they immediately reported that "the U.S. must share the blame,"[39] and again on May 30, "[The] U.S. should be held responsible."[40] Then on May 29, there was a clear shift in reporting, and they began gross exaggerations, stating in the *Nodong Sinmun*, a daily newspaper, "girls and boys were hung from trees, a seven-year old child was taken to a torture room. . . ,"[41] and finally, "History has never seen such an instance of terrible massacre committed in a few days in one city as in Kwangju."[42] Since 1980, few North Korean publications fail to mention the Kwangju Uprising, incorporating it into novels, essays, and political commentary. Most of the accounts are greatly exaggerated. A short story in a recent issue of *Korea Today*, a North Korean magazine published in English provides this example: "The paratroopers were thrilled to see the blood spilt by thrusting their daggers into the naked woman tied to the tree. . . . Where is our savior, cried the heartbroken mother. She looked over the northern sky with clear expectant eyes."[43]

The South Korean reports of the incident minimized and greatly distorted the event by mixing truths and half-truths. On May 21, the following appeared: "Six hundred students started the demonstration, and due to wild rumors exacerbating local sentiments, enraged citizens joined the demonstration."[44] Details indicating the gravity of the event were not reported to the Korean public until May 22, when the Martial Law Command belatedly announced "that a riot which began last Sunday was still out of control."[45] Throughout the ten days, the deaths of soldiers and police were emphasized and those of citizens downplayed. A newspaper of May 21 stated, "As of the morning of the 21st, five policemen and soldiers and one citizen were dead, thirty-four police and soldiers wounded. The soldier was killed when a car was rammed into him."[46] The excesses of the soldiers were never mentioned. Rather reports insisted that "A peaceful demonstration was disrupted by a considerable number of impure elements and hooligans from other regions."[47] Throughout the uprising the government attempted to fix blame on Kim Dae Jung, who had already been arrested on other charges. On May 21, Korean television announced, "Kim Dae Jung's manipulation of recent events speculated."[48] Finally on May 30, the *Korea Herald* proclaimed, "Life returns to normal in Kwangju. Government to show maximum leniency."[49]

The Korean Government Report

On June 1, 1980, the Martial Law Command (MLC) reported that the authorities had determined that "students at Choson and Chonnam Universities in Kwangju, manipulated and agitated by Kim Dae Jung, led demonstrations in the provincial capital which led to a violent riot. North Korean agents also played a part in the riot, along with impure elements cooperating with them."[50] On July 5, 1980, a more comprehensive report was issued charging that Kim Dae Jung was the behind-the-scenes controller of the Kwangju Incident, financing and organizing the bloody rioting. A number of students, considered central to the resistance, were allegedly manipulated by a group of older citizens who acted as "go-betweens" in passing orders from Kim Dae Jung. In particular, according to the MLC, Kim gave five million wŏn [about eight thousand dollars] in demonstration funds to Chong Tong-nyon of Chonnam University, thus "instigating Chong to trigger the May 18 student demonstrations which led to the bloody ten day riot." The report continues, "On May 18 Kim dispatched about forty hoodlums from Seoul to Kwangju, who, disguised as demonstrators, attacked policemen with kitchen knives, hoes, and iron bars and then destroyed or set fire to public buildings. In addition, ten private underlings of Kim infiltrated into Kwangju to spread malicious rumors."[51]

Despite widespread public skepticism, except for minor details, the government has never revised the original report. In August of 1980, the U.S. Embassy issued a public statement calling the charges "far-fetched."[52] Five years later, on June 8, 1985, largely due to persistent calls by the opposition for an investigation, Defense Minister Yun Sòngmin finally reported on the Kwangju Incident to a National Assembly panel. He testified that:

The nine day Kwangju incident was originated by clashes between martial law troops and demonstrators that took place in the course of having brought under control radical demonstrations ignited by some Chŏnnam University students throwing stones against martial law forces. However, the incident worsened extremely as impure elements from outside the city touched off the regional emotion of the citizens and excited them through subtle instigation, spreading groundless rumors, and wirepulling behind the scenes. The military restrained itself to the last moment from exercising its minimum self-defense right to prevent possible injury to citizens even in the state of anarchy created by armed rioters. The military concentrated all its efforts on preventing the situation from growing worse, even if soldiers were massacred mercilessly by rioters. Behind the Kwangju incident was wirepulling by some political forces. This was plainly confirmed in a ruling by the Supreme Court."[53]

This is apparently an allusion to the fact that Kim Dae Jung was subsequently convicted of sedition and sentenced to death.[54]

Conclusions

Central to the government report and deserving special attention is the assertion that the crowd was incited by "political wirepullers" and "impure elements from outside the city" through subtle instigation and groundless rumors. A careful reading of the available accounts, including the government report, would seem to counter this claim decisively. For purposes of clarity I will divide the afternoon of May 18 into two phases. The first phase of the demonstration extends until three, and the second begins at three, when the decision to send in the airborne units was made.

As previously indicated, the initial gathering of people was largely due to the significant fact that the demonstration took place in a crowded downtown area. The government report, however, contends from the very beginning that outside forces incited the people to gather and resist: "From around *noon* (my emphasis) on May 18, there were various groundless rumors prevailing to irritate the sentiment of citizens born in Chŏlla province."[55] This statement indicates that if there were, in fact, outside instigators, they somehow must have been privy to the government plan to use military force, because at noon on May 18, and up until three, the only soldiers in downtown Kwangju were the local combat police. Even the government report states that the rumors which "irritated" the sentiment of the Cholla people were concerned with the use of special forces from Kyŏngsang Province. Although the number of active participants did gradually increase, there was no evidence of certain individuals emerging and trying to rally the crowd. Furthermore, the student from Chonnam University who had allegedly masterminded the uprising at the instigation of Kim Dae Jung was already in custody on other charges.[56]

Indeed, studies of crowd behavior have shown that "there is often a paucity of emergent leadership in a crowd."[57] The response of the largely indifferent crowd was more a reaction to the actions of the combat police than to any emergent agitators. The initial confrontation seemed to follow the classic pattern of mass violence suggested by Roger Brown:

People arrive on the scene with a variety of motivations behind their presence ranging from passionate commitment to simple curiosity. Some are able to articulate their feelings but for many if not most, motivations and fears are dimly focused, barely intruding on consciousness. The aggregate result is a large group of ambivalent people and a collective lack of direction.[58]

This is an apt description of the type of crowd we observed on May 18.

Brown divides crowds into two groups, agitators and followers. Using his terminology, the students would be classified as agitators, but they would not be, as the government contends, "impure elements from outside the city." Furthermore, though the students took the initiative by throwing stones, they could not be considered leaders of the much larger group of onlookers. The great majority of people in downtown Kwangju that afternoon would have to be considered interested but ambivalent followers. Most people were standing on the sidewalks simply watching the students and combat police throw stones at each other and, before three, the main impetus for more active involvement was the excessive use of tear gas.

Our observations would also seem to support Sam Wright's assertion that "Crown action often occurs at too rapid a rate for rumors to be even a small factor."[59] The demonstration of May 18 lasted only about four hours. In the constant movement of the crowd, there was little time to group and discuss the rapidly changing situation; people were reacting too fast. Except for a small number of students, most of the people were reacting on the spot to events they were witnessing first-hand, and were not, incited by rumors, coming into the city from outlying areas.

The fact that more and more people directly involved themselves in the demonstration is not surprising. The followers constantly balanced their "tally sheets," as described by Richard Berk.[60] Many withdrew but, as predicted by studies of crowd behavior, many others decided that action was necessary to protect their perceived interests. In short, they saw their behavior as legitimate. During the entire first phase of the demonstration up until three o'clock, the people simply sparred with the combat police. The crowd did not seem more violent or uncontrollable than in any of the numerous demonstrations that we had witnessed before in Seoul, and certainly less violent than in the riots in Pusan and Masan the previous October.

At three o'clock there was a conspicuous shift in military strategy with the introduction of the special forces. This move dramatically altered the situation and, I feel, is the crucial factor in understanding the broadbased and active support of the people of Kwangju for those who resisted. Within two days the relatively small number of demonstrators initially participating quickly widened to include nearly one-hundred thousand people. When the troopers charged at three and violently subdued the comparatively small crowd, they were able to effect a temporary calm, but they had encouraged a much more serious cycle of violence which spun completely out of control in the coming days. Followers quickly became agitators, rumors (and not from outside the city) began circulating, and many concluded that a violent response to the military was legitimate and justified.

The events of the next day, Monday the 19th, merely added fuel to an already white-hot fire. As eyewitnesses relate, the airborne units continued to use brute force and violence in a bald attempt to control and intimidate people. The strategy of walking through residential areas and selecting young men and beating them was particularly offensive. No amount of "subtle instigation, rumors, or wirepulling" could have been as effective in aggravating the situation as the violence by the soldiers which literally thousands of people directly witnessed.

The government report also claimed that forty hoodlums were sent to Kwangju by Kim Dae Jung on May 18, and that they attacked police-men with kitchen knives, hoes, and iron bars. There is no way for me to verify that statement. However, I was in the center of the demonstration all day Sunday and most of Monday, and I never once saw the demon-strators use anything but stones, not unusual for demonstrations in Korea. None of the eyewitness accounts make any mention of demon-strators attacking police with knives, hoes, or iron bars. Of course, by Tuesday afternoon many people had begun to defend themselves with such implements, but by then the confrontations of the first two days had turned into a full-scale rebellion, no longer confined to students or hoodlums.

The eyewitness accounts of the missionaries and Peace Corps volunteers indicate that the military's claims to have "restrained itself to the last from exercising its minimum self-defense right" and to have "concentrated all its efforts on preventing the situation from growing worse" are spurious at best. All accounts agree that on Sunday, May 18, the paratroopers came into Kwangju at 3 P.M. apparently already having been given orders to use their clubs to control the demonstrators. Re-straint does not describe their use of force. Even during prior demonstra-tions in Seoul, when nearly one-hundred thousand students had flooded the streets, the combat police had been much more cautious and re-strained than they were in Kwangju.[61] From the onset of the demonstra-tion until the order to use force was given, only four hours had elapsed. Whether the order to use force was meant to intimidate or provoke the crowd is a matter of some debate, but as it is inconceivable that the well-disciplined Korean soldiers would act independently, that order must have been given.

Subsequent events were a direct result of this order. It is highly unlikely that the students could have garnered so much popular support for their political demands if the people had not seen the brutality of the troops with their own eyes. The Korean Broadcasting System aggra-vated the situation by incorrect and distorted reporting that further angered the people. The "groundless rumors" would have had no cre-dence if only a few had been subject to the brutality. Many of the rumors probably were not, in fact, true, but people who had just wit-nessed inexplicable and arbitary beatings were much more likely to trust the students, their fellow citizens, and friends than the government—a government that was widely believed to be an extension of the military. When the military acted so brutally, criticism of the political system and those in power became inevitable.

All accounts seem to point to a miscalculation or deliberate pro-vocation by the military. Without access to Korean military records, it remains impossible to make any categorical statements, but we can speculate on their decision to use force. Martial law had just been declared the previous evening, and the authorities were confronted with the first real challenge to their power. They may have felt that a decisive show of force was necessary to discourage any other would-be demonstrators and to display their determination to keep order.

Perhaps they were trying to prevent a repeat of the crisis which had developed in Pusan and Masan the previous October. The doctors at the hospital where I worked were told on Monday the 19th by the commander in charge of military operations for Kwangju that the same tactics that had been used then would be used to control the demonstrators. In those earlier situations, a massive display of brute force had been used to intimidate the people.[62] If that was in fact the strategy, the military either underestimated the consequences of such an excessive show of force, or the soldiers carried out their orders a little too zealously.

A deliberate provocation by the military, though unlikely and difficult to prove, is supported to some extent by circumstantial evidence. In the wake of the Kwangju Incident, attention was focused on the events after, and not prior, to May 18th. The fact that a de facto military coup d'etat had taken place on the night of May 17, with the arrest of most of the major politicians as well as hundreds of student and religious leaders, has been obscured by the turmoil following the Kwangju uprising. Kim Dae Jung, though already in custody before the incident began, was charged with masterminding the uprising and was found guilty. Other students, particularly Chong Tong-nyon from Chonnam University, were also charged with sedition ex post facto.[63] Some human rights organizations charge that the military created a crisis to legitimize intervention in the political process and to justify the arrest of opposition leader Kim Dae Jung.[64] On this analysis, Kwangju was chosen for two reasons; one, the area is Kim's home turf, and two, due to regional prejudices the people of Kwangju would not get much sympathy from the rest of the country.

Whatever the reasons for the ensuing violence, it is fairly evident that the initial resistance, as well as the harsh governmental reaction, was at least partly a consequence of the May 17 coup. As Hannah Arendt notes, "Those who hold power and feel it slipping from their hands, have always found it difficult to resist the temptation to substitute violence for it."[65] Does this statement accurately reflect the political situation in Korea in the spring of 1980? Prior to the uprising the military had in fact been in some danger of losing political power. Elections had been promised, the Yusin constitution had been dismantled, and for the first time in nearly twenty years the possibility was quite good that someone outside of the military would be elected president. The military was uncomfortable with the forces unleashed in the liberal atmosphere that developed following President Park's assassination, and clearly wanted a change in state policy. The defense minister's assessment of the months preceding the uprising reveal this attitude: "campus and labor unrest were a result of an undermined security posture."[66] When the coup took place on the night of May 17, the military was overtly reasserting its hold on power and its determination to change state policy. Met with opposition, they struck with force and violence. The result was predictable. Though the "rebels" managed to hold Kwangju for six days the outcome was hardly in doubt.

Their victory, however, may yet prove Pyrrhic. Arendt observes that "to substitute violence for power can bring victory, but the price is very high, for it is paid not only by the vanquished, it is also paid by the victor in terms of his own power."[67] Since the Kwangju uprising, the legitimacy of the present government has continually been challenged by religious and labor organizations as well as by the traditional opponents, the students. The violent demonstration at Kŏn'guk University in late October of 1986 aptly illustrates the precarious position of the government. Without a thorough investigation of the Kwangju uprising, claims to legitimacy will continue to be summarily dismissed, but it appears unlikely that the government can conduct an open and impartial inquiry without indicting itself.

The Kwangju Incident is widely considered to be a watershed in modern Korean politics. Nonetheless, at this point, it is still impossible to state conclusively the reasons for the uprising. There were many factors involved, and if a clearer picture is to emerge, the military must be more forthcoming and more eyewitness accounts must be documented and verified. It seems evident that the level and brutality of the force employed by the special units during the initial deployment of May 18 and May 19 was completely out of proportion to the level of the demonstration. Yet the government reports never once acknowledge the possibility that the soldiers used excessive force, nor have they been very clear as to who was responsible for the initial decision to use force. They have focused almost entirely on the excesses of the enraged citizens, but have failed to explain adequately or convincingly why the citizens were so enraged. To insist that rumors alone were enough to incite nearly one-hundred thousand people to armed rebellion does not appear to be born out by either facts or reason. On the other hand, human rights groups have continued to present undocumented and unverified reports of indescribable savagery as fact, and seem to miss the point that the number of deaths is to some degree irrelevant; even one death is too many.

The lack of an open, unbiased investigation has already resulted in a great deal of confusion. In the minds of many, the Kwangju uprising and the coup d'etat of May 17 have become so entangled that they are inseparable. The considerable diplomatic and economic achievements of the present government continue to be overshadowed by the repugnance people feel for the means by which the regime came to power. There is thus an urgent need for a more even-handed report complete with facts, figures, and information from the hospitals of Kwangju (including the military hospital), the records of troop movements, and those reports from citizens of Kwangju that can be independently verified. The prospects for such a report are, of course, not good, but until that time the events of those ten days will remain shrouded in secrecy, contradictions, and controversy that will only lead to further misunderstanding, violence, and suffering.

NOTES

1. For an account of the evolution and historical role of regionalism in Korea, see Ki-baik Lee, *A New History of Korea* (Cambridge, Massachusetts: Harvard University Press, 1984), especially pages 66–71, 98–101, and 221–223.

2. For comprehensive studies on factionalism in the nationalist and communist movements, see Chong-sik Lee, *The Politics of Korean Nationalism* (Berkeley: University of California Press, 1963), and Dae-Sook Suh, *The Korean Communist Movement, 1918–1948* (Princeton: Princeton University Press, 1967).

3. *Korean Reader* (Seoul: Yonsei University Press, 1979), pp. 18–22.

4. For further information on Kim's victory, see Ron Richardson, "The Opposition Gets Tough," *Far Eastern Economic Review*, June 8, 1979, p. 12.

5. *Korea Times*, October 6, 1979, p. 1.

6. *Korea Times*, October 7, 1979, p. 1.

7. For an account of these demonstrations, see *Newsweek*, October 29, 1979, pp. 50–51.

8. *Korea Times*, October 27, 1979, p. 1.

9. For an account of the 12/12 Incident, see *Time*, December 24, 1979.

10. "South Korean Army Rears Up," *Time*, December 24, 1979, p. 30

11. The Yusin Constitution was promulgated by President Park in 1972 to prolong his stay in power. For further information, see Young Whan Kihl, *Politics and Policies in Divided Korea* (Boulder: Westview Press, 1984), pp. 59–65.

12. Young Whan Kihl, "Korea's Fifth Republic: Domestic Political Trends," *Journal of Northeast Asian Studies* vol. 1, 1982, pp. 38–40.

13. The first two were and still are opposition leaders, and Kim Jong-pil was the leader of the Democratic Republic Party (DRP).

14. Ron Richardson, *Far Eastern Economic Review*. April 18, 1980, p. 6

15. Paul Courtright, "Eyewitness Account of Demonstrations in Seoul and Kwangju," Unpublished, June 1980.

16. Ron Richardson, "Barricades on the Road to Democracy," *Far Eastern Economic Review*, May 23, 1980, p. 8.

17. Martha Huntley, "Recollections of the Kwangju Uprising: An Eyewitness Account," March, 1985, p. 1.

18. Ron Richardson, "Barricades on the Road to Democracy," p. 8.

19. Armored Personnel Carriers are usually used by combat police to spray demonstrators with a pepper fog.

20. *Korea Times*, June 8, p. 5.

21. Airborne paratroopers are an elite commando group within the Korean military that are given special training in guerrilla warfare tactics.

22. Courtright, p. 3.

23. Huntley, p. 5.

24. Taken from the unpublished accounts of Peace Corps volunteers Judi Chamberlin, David Dolinger, Paul Courtright, and myself, as well as the missionaries Mr. and Mrs. Betts Huntley.

25. Huntley, p. 4.

26. Courtright, p. 3.

27. Judi Chamberlin, "Eyewitness Account of the Kwangju Uprising," Unpublished, p. 5.

28. *Korea Times*, May 27, 1980, p. 1.

29. United States General Wickham was the UN commander in Korea in 1980, and it was widely believed that his permission was necessary to move Korean troops from the Demilitarized Zone to help quell the uprising. For a related story on emerging anti-American sentiment in Korea, see *Time*, June 3, 1985, p. 34.

30. The Blue House is Korea's presidential residence, similar to America's White House.

31. Dolinger, p. 5.

32. For other accounts, see Asia Watch Committee, *Human Rights in Korea* (New York: Asia Watch, 1986), and *Korea Scope*. June–July 1980. *Korea Scope* is a magazine published by the International Christian Network for Democracy in Korea, headquartered in New York.

33. Foreign Broadcast Information Service (FBIS), *TASS*, May 21, 1980.

34. FBIS, *TASS*, June 2, 1980.

35. FBIS, *TASS*, May 25, 1980.

36. FBIS, *People's Daily*, May 22, 1980.

37. FBIS, *Beijing Review*, June 5, 1980.

38. FBIS, *Korea Central News Agency (KCNA)*, May 19, 1980.

39. FBIS, *KCNA*, May 19, 1980.

40. FBIS, *KCNA*, May 30, 1980.

41. FBIS, *Nodong Sinmun*, May 29, 1980.

42. FBIS, *Nodong Sinmun*, May 29, 1980.

43. "Mount Mudung," *Korea Today*, November 11, 1985, p. 51.

44. FBIS, *News Service*, May 21, 1980.

45. *Korea Times*, May 22, 1980.

46. FBIS, *News Service*, May 21, 1980.

47. *Korea Times*, June 1, 1980, p. 1.

48. FBIS, *Korean Television*, May 21, 1980.

49. *Korea Herald*, May 30, 1980, p. 1.

50. *Korea Times*, June 1, 1980, p. 1.

51. *Korea Times*, July 5, 1980, p. 1.

52. *Time*, August 25, 1980, p. 40.

53. *Korea Times*, June 8, 1980, pp. 1–5.

54. His sentence was commuted to twenty years and eventually he was allowed to travel to the United States for medical treatment. Kim returned to Korea in February of 1985 and has been under house arrest on and off since that time.

55. *Korea Times*, June 8, 1985, p. 5.

56. *Korea Scope*, June–July 1980.

57. Sam Wright, *Crowds and Riots: A Study in Social Organization* (Beverly Hills, London: Sage Publications, 1978), p. 61.

58. Roger Brown, *Social Psychology* (New York: The Free Press, 1965), Chapter 4.

59. Wright, p. 24.

60. Cited in *Collective Violence*, ed. James F. Short, Jr. and Marvin E. Wolfgang (Chicago: Aldine-Atherton, 1972), p. 313.

61. Courtright, p. 2.

62. See *Time*, October 29, 1979, p. 60.

63. "Letter From Kwangju," *Far Eastern Economic Review*, May 29, 1981, p. 78.

64. For a more complete discussion, see *Korea Scope*, June–July 1980.

65. Hannah Arendt, *On Violence* (New York: Harcourt, Brace and World, 1969), p. 87.

66. *Korea Times*, June 8, 1985, p. 5.
67. Arendt, p. 53.

SELECTED BIBLIOGRAPHY

Books

Arendt, Hannah. *On Violence*. New York: Harcourt, Brace, and World, 1969.

Asia Watch Committee. *Human Rights in Korea*. New York: Asia Watch, 1986.

Brown, Roger. *Social Psychology*. New York: The Free Press, 1965.

Cumings, Bruce. *The Origins of the Korean War: Liberation and the Emergence of Separate Regimes, 1945-1947*. Princeton, New Jersey: Princeton University Press, 1981.

Friedrich, Carl J. *Revolution*. New York: Atherton Press, 1967.

Hinton, Harold C. *Korea Under New Leadership: The Fifth Republic*. New York: Praeger, 1983.

Kihl, Young Whan. *Politics and Policies in Divided Korea: Regimes in Contest*. Boulder, Colorado: Westview Press, 1984.

Lee, Chŏng-sik. *The Politics of Korean Nationalism*. Berkeley and Los Angeles, California: University of California Press, 1965.

Lee, Ki-baik. *A New History of Korea*. Cambridge, Massachusetts: Harvard University Press, 1984.

Leiden, Carl and Karl M. Schmitt. *The Politics of Violence: Revolution in the Modern World*. Englewood Cliffs, New Jersey: Prentice-Hall, 1968.

Short, James F., Jr. and Marvin E. Wolfgang. *Collective Violence*. Chicago, Illinois and New York: Aldine-Atherton, 1972.

Suh, Dae-Sook. *The Korean Communist Movement, 1918-1948*. Princeton, New Jersey: Princeton University Press, 1967.

Wright, Sam. *Crowds and Riots: A Study in Social Organization*. Beverly Hills, California and London, England: Sage Publications, 1979.

Magazines

"Campus Clash." *Time*. November 10, 1986.

"Chun: A Shadowy Strongman." *Time*. June 2, 1980.

Kihl, Young Whan. "Korea's Fifth Republic: Domestic Political Trends," *Journal of Northeast Asian Studies*, vol. 1 (1982).

"Letter from Kwangju," *Far Eastern Economic Review*. May 29, 1981.

Richardson, Ron. "Barricades on the Road to Democracy," *Far Eastern Economic Review*. May 23, 1980.

"Season of Spleen." *Time*. June 2, 1980.

"South Korea: Ten Days that Shook Kwangju." *Time*. June 9, 1980.

"South Korea: The Army Rears Up." *Time*. December 24, 1979.

"South Korea: Young Generals, New Loyalties." *Far Eastern Economic Review*. December 24, 1979.

Newspapers

1. English Language

Korea Times. October 6, 1979; October 27, 1979; May 22, 1980; June 8, 1980; July 5, 1980; and June 8, 1985.

2. Korean Language

Dong-A Ilbo. May 15 through June 5, 1980.

Foreign Broadcast Information Service
    China. May 18–June 5, 1980.
    North Korea. May 18–June 30, 1980.
    South Korea. May 16–July 15, 1980.
    Soviet Union. May 18–June 5, 1980.

Unpublished Materials

Chamberlin, Judi. "Eyewitness Account of the Kwangju Uprising." June 1980.

Courtright, Paul. "Eyewitness Account of Demonstrations in Seoul and Kwangju." June 1980.

Dolinger, David. "Eyewitness Account of the Kwangju Uprising." June 1980.

Huntley, Martha. "Recollections of the Kwangju Uprising: An Eyewitness Account." March 1985.

Na, Young-chan. "The Kwangju Uprising." Master's thesis. University of Hawaii. 1985.

Warnberg, Tim. "Eyewitness Account of the Kwangju Uprising." June 1980.

This article was published in Volume 11 of the academic journal Korean Studies in 1987.

Appendix: David's Handwritten Memories

David Dolinger has jotted down notes describing what he witnessed in Kwangju since the morning of May 19, 1980, and over the years he has had a number of opportunities to take his raw notes and write them out in a comprehensible and chronological manner. The following is the statement he submitted to the International Human Rights Law Group in June 1981 for their petition to the United Nations Commission on Human Rights regarding human rights violations in Korea. At times, he was given very short notice to write out these statements and did not always have access to all of his notes. For this particular statement he was asked to spell Kwangju with a 'G'.

(1.)

May I first say that all information contained within this document are facts which I observed first hand.

I first came to South Korea on April 21, 1978 as a member of the United States Peace Corps. Upon arrival I recieved ten weeks of intensive language and cross cultural training in Chungju the provincial capital of South Chung Cheong Province. I was sworn in as a Peace Corps Volunteer on June 29, 1978. On July 6 I began me duties as a Tuberculosis control worker in South Cholla Province, Yeongam County Health Center, (Yeongam being located 56 Km southeast of Gwangju). I was a volunteer in Yeongam until June 11, 1980 when I was told by the Peace Corps country director to submit a letter asking for early completion of service (I should have completed on July 30, 1981 because I had been granted a one year extension of service).

On May 15, 1980 the students ~~had agr~~ thru out Korea had agreed to return to the campuses and to stop demonstrating. This was as a result of an appeal made jointly by Kim Dae Jung and Kim Jong Pil. The cities threw out Korea were quiet Friday May 16. The night of May 16 the people of Gwangju (approximately 2000 people) held a candle light march from Gwangju Railroad Station to the Medical school of Chonnam University to show the wish for democracy the march was very peaceful and orderly with the police march at the sides of the marchers.

Saturday was again quiet, and the atmosphere of the city was relaxed; people were hoping for the best. That night martial law was declared along with the arrests of numerous people. The people of Gwangju and Korea awoke sunday May 18 not knowing what had happened only knowing that the hope they had had was no longer real.

That morning when Chonnam students attempted to enter the campus they were deined access by martial law soldiers. The students who did gain access where physically removed often with parts of the clothing remaining on the campus. This happen to female students alike, soldiers attemiting to remove them often had the shirts torn, some even had their shirts ripped off their backs.

Because the students were denied access to their campus (which by law the soldiers were not allowed to ente the met in a market place in Dae In Dong (this was also spurred by the fact that a student was bayonetted to deat while trying to enter the campus; I did not witness the bayoneting). Because of these facts and others (declaration of martial law, arrest of Kim Dae Jung) the students decided to march and let the city know how the felt.

At a approximatly 12:30 about 200 students came marching out of an alley in Dae In Dong marching towards Geum Ro the mayor street of Gwangju. As they marched the sang that "Chun Doo Whan must resign" and that Kim Dae Jung must be released. At Geum Ro the marchers faced off with martial law soldiers. At first it appeare that that was all that was going to happen no violence

For some reason the martial law soldiers started shouting at the students and the crowd, (at this tim the martial law troops commanded Geum Ro with the marchers and onlookers in the side streets and on the side walk. The students and onlookers then picked up stones from a construction site (they were building an underground shopping mall, under Geum Ro) and started throwing them at the troops. To make matters worse the troops started taunting the people by running in front of the other troops and waving the hands. Officers were also ordering their men to do it

Then with out warning the troops attacked (in unison). (This is very strange as the troops were in groups on Guem Ro, a group at the mouth of the major streets opening on to Guem Ro.) The soldiers used their billy club to attack the people hitting anyone that they caught. They even went into stores hitting everyone in the store before leaving. The hitting and beatings were indiscrimi

Those people which the troops decided to hold (usually those most severly beaten) were forced into the middle of Guem Ro where they were forced into trucks with billy clubs. If they slowed at all they were beaten even more, some had to be thrown into the trucks, with their heads split open. By about 3:30 pm the worst was over, the troops were back on Guem Ro with the people in the side streets. Curfew was at 9:00 pm.

Monday morning I returned to Yeougam and did not return to Gwangju until May 21, Buddha's Birthday. I walked from Naju to Gwangju, it took about it took about 5 hours to walk the 24 km.

I arrived on the outskirts of Gwangju at about 3:30 pm where I met a person I knew and we walked into the downtown. Along the way we saw the dead body of a man who had been shot in the chest. His body was on the hood of a military jeep, he was being shown to the people to show them that the death and horror were real. He was being shown by fellow citizens.

As we neared downtown I heard a helicopter, with its approach I saw people in the streets run for cover. I was told that the troops had been flying over since morning and shooting into the crowds. I then saw it myself as a helicopter flew over downtown I saw a soldier lean out of the side door and fire a gun. On thursday when I visited the major hospitals I saw those wounded by the fire. All had wounds of the upper torso with the projectile trajectory going downwards.

When I reached downtown I saw Guem Ro jammed with people, you could barely move on the sidewalks. The soldiers were in front of the provincial offices.

At around 5:30 I returned downtown, at most a five minute walk from where I stayed. On the way I was directed to a private clinic where I saw three young men in the treatment room. They were suffering from gun shot wounds and bayonet wounds. One patient had three bayonet wounds, two in his chest and one in his arm.

From Guem Ro sporatic gun fire could be heard. As I neared I saw that the people were no longer in the street but were in the side streets peering around the building corners. When I peered around I saw a tank parked in front of the Gwangju Bank opposite the Cheil Bank. The soldiers were also shooting up the street so as to keep everyone off of it. The machine gun on the tank was used. This gun fire was sporatic and did not seemed to be directed at anyone.

That night the troops withdrew and the citizens of Gwangju controlled their own city.

Thursday May 22 was a day of happiness, but also a day of worry, pain, sorrow but most of all a day of organizing from Thursday until Monday May 26 (the soldiers retook the city early Tuesday May 27) I spent my time visiting the hospitals, translating for foreign reporters and also in the provincial offices with my friends who were deeply envolved with what was going on.

When the soldiers retook the city I counted 14 tanks, 4 armoured personel carriers, 1 flame throw which was carried by a soldier in the provincial office.

During the Gwangju Incident I was able to talk with the soldiers envolved, they stated that the only reason that they were doing what they were doing was because they were ordered and because the people envolved were communists. They were not drugged nor starved. The black berets the soldiers envolved, are taught to kill

AND OBEY NOTHING ELSE. FROM A SOURCE WHO WORKED FOR THE KOREAN ARMY I WAS TOLD THAT ALOT OF THE OFFICERS IN CHARGE WERE FROM THE CHOLLA PROVINCIAL AREA AND WERE USED BECAUSE THEY HAD TO SHOW THEIR LOYALTY TO THE GOVERNMENT AND WOULD BE HARDER ON THEIR OWN PEOPLE

ABOUT THOSE KILLED MY OWN ESTIMATIONS ARE THAT BETWEEN 1000 AND 1500 PEOPLE WERE KILLED (FROM WHAT I OBSERVED, AND FROM WHAT I KNOW). BUT THIS FIGURE IS VERY HARD TO COME UP WITH BECAUSE THE SOLDIERS DID TAKE AWAY LARGE NUMBERS OF WOUNDED, AND MANY PEOPLE ARE STILL MISSING. BUT IT CAN BE SAID THAT OF THE POPULATION IN GWANGJU (OVER ONE MILLION) ALL HAVE SUFFERED A LOSS EITHER RELATIVE OR FRIEND.

WHILE THE CITIZENS CONTROLED GWANGJU THOSE IN CHARGE OPENED THE POLICE GYMNASIUM SO THAT 67 CASKETS COULD BE DISPLAYED AND MEMORIAL SERVICES COULD BE HELD, THE AGE RANGED FROM A FOUR YEAR OLD TO A 67 YEAR OLD GRANDFATHER, BOTH MALE AND FEMALE, STUDENT AND WORKER.

LET IT BE KNOWN THAT THE CITIZENS PLANNED IN BURYING THESE IN THE GYMNASIUM ON SUNDAY MAY 25. BUT THE MARTIAL LAW COMMAND WOULD NOT ALLOW IT. ~~THIS~~ ~~AS THE AGREEMENT BETWEEN THE CITY~~ ONE OF THE DEMANDS OF THE MARTIAL LAW COMMAND WAS TO RETAIN ALL BODIES FOR AUTOPSY. SO THE GWANGJU DEAD WERE NOT BURIED WHEN THEY SHOULD HAVE BEEN BY KOREAN CUSTOMS.

LET IT ALSO BE KNOWN THAT THE CITIZENS IN CHARGE WANTED A PEACEFUL SETTLEMENT, BUT KNEW THAT THE SOLDIERS WOULD ATTACK AND THAT THEY LIVES WOULD BE SACRIFICED.

TO THE BEST OF MY KNOWLEDGE EVERYTHING STATED IN THIS DOCUMENT IS A FACT WITNESSED BY ME.

7/8/81

Cleora E. Clark
Phila., Pa

CLEORA E. CLARK
Notary Public, Phila., Phila. Co.
My Commission Expires Jan. 2, 1983

David Dolinger
DAVID DOLINGER

Acknowledgements

No book is written without a great deal of help from a variety of people. The authors would jointly like to thank Jon Dunbar and Jacco Zwetsloot, who read and copy-edited a draft of the manuscript and provided insightful suggestions, and Suzanne Crowder Han, who copy-edited the final manuscript. For their contributions to the chapter "Remembering Tim," we would like to thank Roxanne Wilson, Keevie Fairbanks, Paul Courtright, Susan Cunningham-Jopling, Noren Lush, Robert Grotjohn, Angie Huse, Terry Anderson, and Gerry Bevers. Many thanks must go to Choi Yong-ju for translating the book into Korean. And, of course, we would like to thank our publisher, Park So-yeon, who provided encouragement and advice, invigorated us when we were less-than-motivated, patiently completed a long list of necessary tasks, and got us over the finish line as deadlines loomed.

David Dolinger

This never would have happened without Matt, who listened to my stories and thoughts, brought insight and mental stimulation, and truly helped this old scientist write a story that wasn't data-driven and sterile. Thanks also to Marcy Lynne and Tim Shorrock for their discussions, encouragement, and support.

I would like to thank all those who were with me during May of 1980. You were the people that made me flower, who led me to try to focus my life on others, just as you did during those fateful days.

Matt VanVolkenburg

I would like to thank Martha Huntley and Barbara Peterson for sharing their memories of 5.18 with me, and Steve Literati for sharing material from the University of Southern California's Peace Corps Korea Archive. Thanks also to former PCVs Suzanne Crowder Han, Tom Coyner, and the late Peter Bartholomew for sharing stories of their Peace Corps service over the years. Last, but not least, I thank my parents, Wayne and Cathy, and my sister, Jane, for their love and support through the years.

Publisher Goggas
would like to thank
Kickstarter backers
for being part of the
journey.

---

*Backers' names are in alphabetical order.

Beth A. Sanders
Bryan Hale
Cathy Park
Chandrasekhar Nair
Christoph David Hohl
Cody Tornow
David Butterworth
Don Baker
Eom Hye Young
Frank Murphy
Gary Hedrick
Guy Lambinon
Heinz Reiske
Isaiah Whisner
James Mahon
Janey DeSales Whalen
Jason Smith
jt sauls
Kim Eun Gyong
Marcy Tanter
Margaret Love
Michael S Daines
Otto Silver
Park Hanjin
Paul Matthews
Robert J. Dickey
Ryan Berkebile
Shannon Paquette
Tobi
Wilson Keng
하민성 (Milan Hejtmanek)

and others who wished to remain
anonymous

DAVID LEE DOLINGER

AUTHOR

David has a Ph.D. in Microbiology and Immunology from Temple University Medical School and has been developing tests for human diseases, particularly infectious diseases, for more than thirty five years. He has worked in various positions for multiple companies, large and small, and has developed an extensive knowledge concerning the design, development and commercialization of in vitro diagnostic tests and instrumentation.

David first arrived in Korea in April of 1978 as a Peace Corps volunteer. His Korean name is Im Dae-oon, which was given to him by his Korean teachers when he first came to Korea. In Korean, his family name, Im, means 'Forest,' and his given name, Dae-oon, means 'big cloud.' His experiences as a Peace Corps Volunteer and the horror and heroism he witnessed in Kwangju in May 1980 set him on a new path and shaped him into the person he is today.

MATT VANVOLKENBURG

CO-AUTHOR

Originally hailing from Canada, Matt first arrived in Korea in 2001. Fascinated by Korea's modern history, in 2005 he began writing about Korean history, society, and culture on his blog, *Gusts of Popular Feeling*. More recently, he supplemented his history degree with an MA in Korean Studies from the University of Washington and is currently researching 1970s Korean youth culture. Having read voraciously about the Gwangju Uprising since 2001, Matt immediately recognized David's name when they met in an online forum in 2006, and the seeds of this book were first planted when they finally met in person seven years later.

www.ingramcontent.com/pod-product-compliance
Lightning Source LLC
Chambersburg PA
CBHW011235120626
46549CB00009B/3276